D1444843

Answers

FROM
Andrew

BY CRISTINA LIBERATI

FORWARD

My dream had always been college, marriage, and kids. From my earliest memories I had wanted a big family; four kids, to be exact. I thought for sure I would have a kindergartner by the time I was thirty. You can only imagine the disappointment of my thirtieth birthday; no husband, no kids, and certainly no kindergartner. Where had my plan gone wrong?

Shortly after I turned thirty I met Tom, an attorney, and a freshly divorced father of two. Not perfect, but hey, you know what they say about, "what the heart wants." It was by any standard a whirlwind romance. Within a year we were married, and I was pregnant with what would be the first of three children for us in a short period of time. I had three kids within three years. That would total five children between the two of us. By the time we had our last baby, we had five kids aged ten and under living in our home. To say that life was hectic, chaotic, and demanding would be an understatement. Even under the most ideal situation, the circumstances were not a recipe for success. Add in the daily stressors of work, life, in-laws, his ex, kids' school and activity schedules, lack of sleep, and my best efforts to keep home life running smoothly, and you can see why even on a good day I was overwhelmed.

During the first few years, my parents were living in Seattle. By the time I had my third baby they had retired to Arizona. As helpful as they were—and trust me, they helped me every day—I'm not sure there was ever enough help. The kids outnumbered the adults. Over time, Tom's two older children began to live with us full time. Our oldest daughter, Isabella, was an extremely bright, demanding child, very set in her schedule and routine. Andrew, our second child, was quiet and preferred to be alone. Last but not least, Sophia, the baby was a preemie, and had respiratory issues on and off throughout her infancy, including several hospitalizations.

As I look back at the journal entries I have kept as long as I can remember, I realize what an idealist I had been about marriage and motherhood. I went from trying to achieve an unrealistic standard to survival mode in a relatively short period of time. For the purposes of this book, my entries pick up after the birth of my first child, Isabella, and upon receiving the news that my second child would be a son.

My hope is that by opening up my journal and my journey with one of my children, my son Andrew, I can offer you something. Maybe up until you read this you felt alone in your journey. You are not alone. Perhaps you have a family member, friend or neighbor raising a special needs child. Hopefully, this can give you a glimpse at what is going on in their home. In my darkest hour, I never gave up hope that my son could achieve great things. While I may have to accept his limitations, I continue to see all the opportunities for growth; both his and mine. Raising Andrew has made me not only a better mother, but a better human. To have the opportunity to see the world through his eyes has made me value love, kindness, compassion, true friendship and, above all else, empathy.

It is an honor and privilege to say, I'm Andrew's mom.

I FORGET TO REMEMBER

As a young woman, long before I was married or had children, I had a mentor that introduced me to a prolific perspective on parenthood. He suggested that children are not our property, that we don't own them. Children merely pass through us. They are not bestowed upon us to fulfill all of our unfulfilled childhood dreams. Our real job is to help our children uncover their area of excellence, and foster and support their development in that direction.

If we enter parenthood with this perspective, we protect ourselves from a lot of unnecessary disappointment. You see, if we embrace this philosophy, we have to let go of the notion that our children will become all of the things that we didn't or haven't. This makes so much sense on an intellectual level, but the truth is, it is very hard.

The reality for myself is that, from the time I found out I was pregnant with each of my children, I began to dream big dreams for them. It's human nature. What do you mean, we don't own our kids? Why do we fight over custody for them when we get divorced? What do you mean they aren't going to be all the things we weren't? Of course one of my kids will play the violin. Why did I choose the oboe again? I know one of them will be an Olympic athlete or a professional one because I have a vision of standing in a stadium proudly crying through the National Anthem. I know they will all get straight As and go to Ivy League schools. And I know that all four of them will be doctors so I can face family, friends and even strangers and know, by their standards, I am a good mom. Despite all my failures and shortcomings, it will appear I have done something right. Right?

Time and time again I have to remind myself: My children are not here to fulfill my unfulfilled childhood dreams. They are here to live their own dreams and their own lives. I'm just here to help make it happen.

I'd forget to remember. Andrew would gently remind me.

BIRTH-AGE 3
2003-2006

IT'S A BOY!

When the doctor told me that I was having a boy, I started to cry. Not the good, happy cry. The ugly, "What am I going to do with a boy?" cry. I felt like I had been sucker-punched. I had a baby girl at home. I have this girl thing down. But a boy? The truth is, I'm not very good at the male/female relationship thing. I have no empirical evidence that I can have a successful relationship with a man, present company included. I mean, how am I going to play with a boy? Do I have to play trucks, and army? Do I have to learn how to make a whole array of noises that have never come out of my mouth? Will I be resigned to potty humor? Last, but not least, what will he wear? After all, we all know there are no cute boy clothes. My mother-in-law told me boys are easier. Really, she only has boys. What is her frame of reference? I knew it would take me a while to wrap my head around the fact that I was having a boy, but my wish for my unborn baby was simple: Healthy!

HAPPY BIRTHDAY

On August 5th my son, Andrew Thomas, arrived into the world the same way he had spent the last nine months; quietly.

My father had the honor of being the first non-medical professional to hold Andrew. Watching him stare into the eyes of his newborn grandson, I could see him soften. It was as if a physical transformation was taking place. I imagine the birth of his first grandson helped in some way to heal the pain of all the broken dreams he had once held for his only son, and that Andrew's birth provided a pathway for new hopes and dreams to find a way into his heart. I hoped that this joyous event he was celebrating with me could help to ease the heartache of the slow death of his son. It had been almost two years since my brother was diagnosed with brain cancer.

When it was my turn, I held my new baby boy, and I was euphoric. All of my fears about having a son dissolved. So on that very special day, my wishes for my son were....

May you have a kind and loving heart.

May you always be humble in the presence of great success.

I hope you pay attention in school and work hard for good grades so that you always have the doors of opportunity open to you.

May you always show respect to others, especially when you don't see eye to eye.

I hope you always have an attitude for gratitude.

I hope you don't find your self-worth in things.

May you learn to love unconditionally and with abandon.

Last, but not least, I hope that you are a nice boy!

All my love, Mom

IT'S A GOOD THING HE'S CUTE

My little man was a miserable baby with a miserable mom. He had COLIC!! He slept 45 minutes and then cried 45 minutes, 24 hours a day. This was no way to live, for either one of us. I had him drinking gripe water by the dropper full. I was starting to think that with all the complaining I was doing maybe I'm the one that needed the gripe water. I alternated between gripe water, MYLICON, homeopathic tummy tablets and, as a last resort, I started feeding him Nutramigen. Talk about sticker shock! To add insult to injury, the Nutramigen, in my opinion, smelled disgusting. My child was now drinking my clothing budget. Maybe that's why I'm so irritated. It couldn't possibly be the lack of sleep. Maybe it was the realization that I was spending all this money on the product that my baby drinks, still cries and then ultimately throws up all over me or craps out, or both at the same time. I think maybe I cried for forty-five minutes over that. Ha! Two can play at this game, Andrew. Actually, I was afraid that if I started to cry, I might not stop. I was overwhelmed. Four kids; Tom's two, our two, no sleep, no help. All that aside, no feeling in the world compared to having Andrew fall asleep on my chest. As I stared down on my miserable little man, I thought to myself, *it's a good thing he's so cute.* It was his saving grace.

THE OVERDUE FLU

I just couldn't seem to shake the flu. I made a doctor's appointment for myself (novel concept) and got a sitter for the kids. Best idea ever! It's too bad I wasn't doing anything fun. It wasn't the flu. I was pregnant. Yes, pregnant with baby number three. Andrew was only nine months old, and Isabella was 18 months old. That would be three kids under three. Not new math, not old math, just REAL math. I could hear Tom come through the door that night from work. He was surprised to find a sitter with the kids, and me in bed. He knew something was wrong. "What's wrong? What did the doctor say?" You could see the concern on his face. "The doctor said I caught the 'Overdue Flu;' I'm pregnant!" As I said the words out loud, I started to cry. Tom started to laugh. Of course he's laughing. He gets to go to work all day. He thinks that this is such a great blessing and can't wait to tell everyone. He wanted to call a family meeting immediately. Put the brakes on that! "You have to give me a chance to wrap my head around the idea before we tell everyone," I insisted. No surprise, I won that. Together with the other two kids, that's five kids. I was just trying to keep my head above water as it is. To say I was overwhelmed was an understatement.

I got my flu shot that year. But, I'm just saying, there was no warning about this immunization being ineffective for the Overdue Flu that's going around.

RADIO SILENCE

All the books say to trust your instincts. Listen to your inner voice. I'm worried about Andrew. He didn't talk. He didn't say anything. I just knew something was wrong. The first time I mentioned it to the pediatrician, he pointed out that my frame of reference was skewed. I knew that most kids didn't start talking at eight months like Isabella. I recognized that she was an anomaly. I also knew that you couldn't compare kids, and I'm really not. I just felt deep in the pit of my stomach that something was not right. He should have been making sounds or something.

For the first few weeks of Andrew's life, he slept about twenty two hours a day. I kept asking if this was normal. The doctor kept reassuring me that each kid is different, and some just need more sleep. Really? Even cats, who are notorious nappers, don't sleep twenty-two hours a day. Well, after numerous concerned phone calls, I finally brought him in, and guess what? I was right. There is a hole in our heart that closes during the birth process, and Andrew's hadn't closed. Guess I wasn't so crazy after all!! Lucky for Andrew, it closed while we were waiting for him to reach eleven pounds, which is the magic weight at which doctors feel comfortable operating on infants.

I kept mentioning that he didn't talk. We'd gone for hearing tests, and he could hear. I wasn't sure how they knew, but they insist they do. At every appointment for any of the kids, I asked if this was normal that he wasn't talking at all, and this is the story I got: "My son was a late talker. Boys are late to talk and late to do a lot of things. He lives with a lot of people who take care of his needs so he doesn't need to talk. Plus, he has a sister who is very talkative," the doctor said. Let's be honest; he lives with a sister who never shuts up. From the minute her eyes were open in the morning, so was her mouth. I had to ask her for five minutes of quiet at the end of the day just to stop her mouth from moving long enough to fall asleep. Back to the doctor's speech: "My son started talking late and now he goes to an Ivy League school. Andrew will be fine."

I just kept wondering; if he doesn't get into that Ivy League school that I keep hearing about, do I get a refund for all the times I had to listen to this speech? This story was no consolation for me. A mother knows. I couldn't shake the feeling. I knew his silence was telling me something.

WHO NEEDS A GYM MEMBERSHIP?

Despite all my concern, the reality is that life keeps going, and so must I. I had kids to feed, errands to run, places to go. I admired the moms that always seemed to be on the go, venturing out into society with their kids. The mere thought was exhausting. In order to go out, I had to organize supplies for three small kids. There were diapers, snacks, a change of clothes, drinks, and entertainment items. It was enough to fill a small suitcase. Next, I had to get all three ready to go. Fresh outfits, fresh diapers, are they fed, clean? Am I? Then there's the trek to the car with kids and stuff in tow. Junk in the trunk first. Then, one by one, I load everyone into the car and into their car seats. Youngest to oldest, and depending on what time of year it is, we had to deal with the Arizona heat. By the time I was backing out of the driveway, I was hot, irritated and wondering where I had to go that was so important.

Once on the road, the drama began. I always had Andrew crying. I had Isabella who wants to chatter non-stop, and baby Sophia, who may cry or try to talk, depending on the circumstances. Then, if a toy got snatched or someone touched someone, I may have to pull the car over to play referee. Why did I want to go somewhere again?

Upon arrival at our destination the fun really began. I had to unload everyone one at a time into the stroller, and then all of the kids' stuff. Who knew you had to travel with so much stuff just to go out of the house when you have kids? But you know the minute you leave home without it, disaster hits, and you end up having to buy it. (Can you say five tubes of DESITIN, three bottles of MYLICON, seven packages of diaper wipes?) You may as well just bring it with you. By the time I had everyone unloaded, I didn't even remember why I'd left the house. Hopefully I wrote it down. How embarrassing is this that I had to write everything down? "Mommy brain" is true. It is not an urban myth. The more kids you have, the less you remember. Who is the president again? In case my nerves weren't on edge by then, they would be. I had Isabella with me who doesn't stop asking questions. Not the kind of questions you can passively listen to; the kind of questions that require answers. Andrew couldn't stand to go anywhere: he only wanted to be at home, so crying spells were predictable. He cried on and off and wanted to be held. As soon as he wanted to be held, Sophia joined in the fun and she wanted to be held too. So picture this: All of my 110 pounds pushing a stroller full of kids' stuff with Isabella in it, Andrew in my other arm and Sophia in the carrier on my chest. I really love the random stranger who would say, "Boy, you've got your hands full." You think? By the way, do you think you could hold that door open for me?

Repeat again, just to go home. Each day I was tired before I even got out of bed. I was emotionally, physically, and mentally exhausted before my feet even hit the floor. My doctor thought I needed a gym membership. I thought I needed a nanny!

HE IS THE DOCTOR

It was "Well Visit" day at the pediatrician's office. Isabella was already four, and Sophia was one. Since Andrew was two and a half, he wouldn't have his visit for six more months, but I dragged him along anyway, since we navigate life as an entourage. That's four of us in a small exam room. Isabella was predictably hiding under the exam table, Andrew was playing trains on the floor and I was holding Sophia on my lap. The pediatrician blew in, did his exam, asked all the usual questions and sent the nurse in to give the immunizations. It was looking good. An in-and-out visit. Isabella predictably flipped out over getting a shot and was crying. Andrew joined in for a sympathy cry, and Sophia didn't shed a tear. We were bee-lining for our well-deserved stickers and suckers when the pediatrician stopped me.

Doctor: Do you think you could bring Andrew back tomorrow, without the girls?

Me: Um, why? He isn't due for his well visit for six more months.

Doctor: Well, I'm concerned about him.

As he hands me the M-CHAT questionnaire he lobs the grenade in.

Doctor: I think he's autistic.

Me: What????

Doctor: I think he's autistic. (He repeated it as if I really didn't hear him the first time.) Fill out the form, come back tomorrow, and we'll talk then.

Discussion over. After all, he is the doctor.

I felt sick.

I LOVE A PASS/FAIL TEST

The Internet said the M-CHAT is used for early detection of autism and pervasive development disorders. This is how the scoring goes for the M-CHAT; a child fails when two or more critical items are failed OR when any three items are failed. Yes/No answers convert to pass/fail responses. I was provided with the answer key for the questions, and any answer in BOLD CAPS is considered a critical item.

1. **Does your child enjoy being swung, bounced on your knee, etc.?**
   YES (Off to a good start.)

2. **Does your child take an interest in other children?**
   NO (Oops. Is this bad? Sometimes I'm not interested in other children. Sometimes other children aren't interesting.) *Note: critical item.

3. **Does your child like climbing on things, such as up stairs?**
   NO (Oh, I thought it was good he was cautious.)

4. **Does your child enjoy playing peek-a-boo/hide-and-seek?**
   NO (Uh-oh.)

5. **Does your child ever pretend, for example, to talk on the phone or take care of dolls, or pretend other things?**
   NO (So...he's not creative.)

6. **Does your child ever use his/her index finger to point, to ask for something?**
   NO (He has never asked me for anything.)

7. **Does your child ever use his/her index finger to point, to indicate interest in something?**
   NO (Houston, we have a problem!! *Critical item.)

8. Can your child play properly with small toys (e.g. cars or bricks) without just mouthing, fiddling, or dropping them?

YES (Andrews got this one, he's amazing with his trains.)

9. Does your child ever bring objects over to you (parent) to show you something?

NO (Not looking so good. *Another critical item.)

10. Does your child look you in the eye for more than a second or two?

NO (I'm officially feeling sick to my stomach.)

11. Does your child ever seem oversensitive to noise? (e.g. plugging ears.)

YES (I can't turn the vacuum on when Andrew's home to save my life.)

12. Does your child smile in response to your face or your smile?

YES (Back on track here. He smiles at me.)

13. Does your child imitate you? (i.e. you make a face-will your child imitate it?)

NO (What's to imitate? I'm not that exciting. *Critical item.)

14. Does your child respond to his/her name when you call?

NO (Bueller?...Bueller?) Ugggh *Critical item.

15. If you point at a toy across the room, does your child look at it?

NO (*Critical item.)

16. Does your child walk?

YES (Things are looking up.)

17. Does your child look at things you are looking at?

NO (Back down.)

18. Does your child make unusual finger movements near his/her face?

YES (When he's excited he flaps like a bird; it looks like he's trying to fly.)

19. **Does your child try to attract your attention to his/her own activity?**

NO (I'm starting to break out into a cold sweat.)

20. **Have you ever wondered if your child is deaf?**

YES (I've already taken him for the hearing test. He passed.)

21. **Does your child understand what people say?**

NO (Actually, I'm not sure, but he doesn't behave like he even hears them.)

22. **Does your child sometimes stare at nothing or wander with no purpose?**

YES (I can't even think of something witty to say.)

23. **Does your child look at your face to check your reaction when faced with something unfamiliar?**

NO

Survey Says: 4 Pass/19 Fail

Up until tonight, I really loved a pass/fail test. Oh, my quirky little kid. How could I have missed the signs?

My son, I have failed you.

THE TRUTH HURTS

As I sat in the silence of nightfall to write in my journal, I felt a different kind of darkness starting to envelop me. I knew before I even took Andrew to our appointment that it was true. I'd sensed for a long time now that something was not quite right, and now it had a label. I could tell that I'd been living with a lawyer for too long because I was already working on my opening statement for this appointment tomorrow.

I just thought he was the strong, silent type. I thought it was a good thing that he could play for hours on end by himself. How great was it that he was so independent? I was so relieved that out of five kids, there was one that never bugged me for anything.

Now I was just embarrassed and ashamed for my lack of observation. It was right in front of me all along and I didn't even notice. How could I not have seen it? What kind of mother am I? A bad one. How did he get it? What is it? What do I do about it? Does this mean he'll never talk? Will he ever tell me he loves me? Does he know how much I love him? I mean, does he really know? Does he even understand what I'm saying when I talk to him?

The pain in my heart was like nothing I'd ever felt before. There was nothing the doctor would tell me the next day that would make me feel any better or any worse. I had failed at the only job that mattered. That was my truth.

AUTISM DEFINED

I bought every book on Autism that Barnes and Noble had in stock. Thirty books later, this is my best summary.

Autism defined by me: Autism affects the brain's normal development of social and communication skills. It is a developmental disorder that appears in the first three years of life.

What autism looked like in Andrew? He couldn't stand loud noises, especially the vacuum cleaner. Who knew I'd ever have a legitimate excuse not to vacuum? He'd cover his ears and start to rock back and forth when any sound was too loud for him. His threshold was not very high. Andrew had limited language skills. I would say none, but technically that is not an accurate statement. He did not respond to eye contact; actually, he avoided eye contact. He rarely smiled. I could get him to smile, but if someone smiled at him, he would not mimic the expression. Thomas The Train and the other engines were Andrew's constant companions. He preferred solitary and ritualistic play. Trains were his only interest. Andrew didn't wear shoes. He performed repeated body movements. Some days he'd flap his arms and hands so hard it looked like he was trying to take off flying. A change in his routine affected him as if it was the end of the world. It could take up to an hour for Andrew to stop crying, even when being consoled. That, in a nut-shell, was what autism looked like to me in Andrew.

How did autism feel? Overwhelming. My heart hurt for him when I knew that a sound was too loud for him, when I couldn't communicate with him and when he couldn't communicate with me. I was sad when his own father couldn't get him to smile or engage. I felt his loneliness when he played by himself in a room full of children. I was frustrated when I couldn't get him to wear shoes, because I knew I was being judged as a mother. I was embarrassed for him when he flapped his arms because I knew what people were thinking. I feel my blood pressure going through the roof when there was a change in our routine and I knew a meltdown was coming on. Autism was isolating not only for Andrew, but for me, too.

SPECIALISTS ARE SPECIAL

My pediatrician confirmed the results of the M-CHAT and without much fanfare, referred us to a specialist. We would need an official diagnosis to be eligible for services through the state. What? Yes, I'd heard that right. Andrew would need an early intervention program, speech therapy, physical therapy, occupational therapy, music therapy, animal therapy, and who knows what else he said to me. I'd lost the plot. The problem was, the best doctors in town had long waiting lists, and they didn't work on Fridays. I really want my kids to grow up to be doctors!

Long story short, our doctor knew another doctor that had left one of the big hospitals to go into private practice doing assessments. One phone call later, we set an appointment for the next day. After lots of tears and hugs, our pediatrician sent us on our way. He warned me that this doctor was good and well respected, but his bedside manner left something to be desired. It was Friday, my 36th birthday. The big appointment day. My mom came over to watch the girls. Andrew was out of his routine and I could tell he was in no mood for the day. The doctor greeted us and took us into his small office. Andrew refused much of the exam. The doctor performed the CAT/CLAMS exam (Cognitive Adaptive Test/ Clinical Linguistic and Auditory Milestone Scale), an assessment taken for identifying and quantifying delays in language and cognition. At the conclusion of the exam, the doctor acknowledged that Andrew had met the criteria for childhood autism. He briskly rose from his desk and escorted us to the lobby. He asked for payment for today's exam. After I paid him, I asked if we needed to make an appointment for a return visit.

Doctor: That will not be necessary. There is no prescription for me to write. There is no pill to cure this.

I felt dizzy and I could taste the bile in my throat. I thought I would either throw up or pass out. I scooped up Andrew and made a quick exit out of the place. I just wanted to go home. After I got Andrew set in his car seat, I took a few minutes to collect myself before I headed home. Suddenly, there was a knock on my window. It was the doctor.

Doctor: I apologize for what must appear as a lack of empathy. You need to call the Division of Developmental Disabilities and tell them I've sent you. Here's the number.

As quickly as he appeared, he disappeared. The pin had been pulled from the grenade and he was on the run. I knew no more about Autism after this visit than I did before I got here.

We were no more than in the driveway when my mom rushed out with the girls to greet us. I just looked at her and nodded my head. It was unspoken, but I knew in her heart she knew. I could see her nose getting red and tears coming to her eyes. I just couldn't say it out loud. I knew if I spoke I would cry and maybe she would, too. In front of the kids was just no place to have this conversation. Mom: Would you like to postpone your birthday dinner? Dad and I will understand.

Me: Let's cancel.
Mom: How was the doctor?
Me: He was special.

WHAT I KNEW FOR SURE

What I knew for sure was that I would have many dark days and nights ahead of me. What I also knew for sure was that while I may have missed all the signs, I had a big job ahead of me and on this, I would not fail. I knew that I had a lot of research and planning to do. I knew that it was imperative for me to have my head in the game. What I knew for sure was that this was a tremendous opportunity for growth. I knew that I expected great things from Andrew, and that he could expect great things from me. I knew that I did not have a plan. But I knew that once I had one, I would implement it with excellence. Like my mom says, "When we know better, we do better." What I knew for sure was that I love my son, and that he can count on me. I will not let him down.

As I had been obsessively worrying about Andrew, the stars must have been moving into alignment, because just the right plan had presented itself. Jeanine's mom (Isabella's little pre-school friend) called one night to ask a favor. She had a conflict and was wondering if Jeanine could come over for a playdate, and her husband would pick her up after work. Are you kidding me? Her dad? Dr. Rho, *THE* Dr. Rho? Head of Pediatric Neurology at Barrows Neurological Institute? Hell, yes, Jeanine can come over!! I knew the opportunity would be there, and in shameless fashion, I was going to ask for his advice.

Dr. Rho couldn't have been more appreciative that we had hosted Jeanine for the day. Truth be told, when you already have a lot of kids, one more is no problem. It's actually helpful. They all entertain each other. As I was listening to his honest gratitude, I wasted no time. I took a deep breath and went for it. Me: So I was wondering if I could ask your advice... (I don't wait for an answer.) Andrew was diagnosed with autism, and I was wondering, if he were your son, where would you go for a second opinion, and what would you do?

Dr. Rho: (Without missing a beat.) I would take him to see Dr. Donnelly, Dr. Joseph Donnelly, at For OC Kids in Southern California. He's the best. Let me give you his number. Tell him I sent you. If you have any problems getting an appointment, let me know. He gave me Dr. Donnelly's number, his own number, and with true sincerity, let me know to please call if he could help in any way. I was armed and dangerous. I called first thing the next morning to make an appointment to see Dr. Donnelly. His staff informed me that he only saw patients that physically live in Orange County, and he was fully booked for this calendar year. What? It's March! Are you kidding me? Not a joke, I'm informed. Next phone call, Dr. Rho. He took my call. Good sign. I replayed the events for him and he said he would make a few phone calls and get back to me by the end of the day. He did better than that. He stopped by my house on his way home. He got us on the cancellation list with Dr. Donnelly. It meant that we would get a one-day notice for an available appointment, and we were expected to take it. In the meantime, he wanted to talk about where I could go and what I should be doing in Arizona to get Andrew help. He gave me a great list of referrals. I already felt better. Not better-better, just I-have-a-plan-in-the-works better.

I was hesitant to ask Dr. Rho, but I couldn't help myself. I just wanted to make sure that I was doing all that I could for Andrew. The waiting lists are so long for all of these services and therapy, it matters who you know. I was at the mercy of other peoples' expertise to get help for Andrew. It was official. In an effort to get the best care possible for Andrew, I would be shameless in my execution of name-dropping and in calling in favors. He deserves it!

My philosophy is, if I take only one thing away from each book, it's been worth reading. Side note: there are some crazy people out there, doing some crazy things. My pediatrician had warned me that there are people out there that will prey on your desperation, and that you need to do your homework before you try any therapy or "procedure." I use that term very loosely. Boy was he right!

The book on mercury had scared me away from seafood. I don't eat it anyway, but I do serve shark (fish sticks) to the kids. I took Andrew in to have his blood tested for metals and he didn't have any, much to my relief. I could scratch that from my list of things to worry about. To immunize or not to immunize? That is the question. I think my pediatrician summed this one up nicely. He said, "No child has ever died from autism. They have, however, died from childhood diseases for which they were not immunized." Point taken. We would immunize, but I thought I would do them one at a time, instead of more than one per appointment.

I had started taking the More Than Words class and working through the workbook. The program is designed to help parents become their child's primary language facilitator. More Than Words offers the best tools, strategies and resources to support parents' involvement in their child's language intervention. This has been very helpful to me. I was finding opportunities to help Andrew ask me for things that in the past I had just taken care of for him. He still wasn't asking me, but he was picking up my cues that he should be doing something. I was trying sign language for the basics, and he could do it. All the other kids had picked up sign language easily and were trying to engage Andrew.

We started physical therapy. The biggest surprise to me was that he couldn't walk up and down stairs. I was in disbelief over this. We didn't have stairs in our home, so I didn't know he couldn't even do this. Until now, I didn't realize how much he couldn't do that he should be able to do. He lacks balance and fine motor skills. There was no nice way to sugarcoat this. I used to justify his clumsiness by saying he was a toddler. Isn't that what it means to be a toddler, to toddle? From the professionals' point of view, the answer to that question is NO, in case you were wondering. Andrew was going to the only speech therapist in town that had an opening. I knew why she had an opening, but I was at her mercy. She wouldn't let him bring his trains into his session. I didn't understand this. I was paying for her to take away the one thing he loves, and cry about it for twenty-five minutes, and work with her for five. This was a waste of my time and money. I didn't understand why the therapy couldn't involve the trains. I was using the trains all the time now. They ate when I wanted him to eat. I thought Percy the Train loved the mac 'n' cheese I make. Thomas the Tank Engine loved to brush his teeth. Henry loved bath time. He even got to go in the tub with Andrew. Last, but not least, all the trains would go into the shed at night, and then Andrew climbed into his bed. I mean, I don't have any initials after my name, but if I could figure all this out, I was sure a qualified professional could develop a speech program for him that involved his trains. I was reading anything I could get my hands on, and I'd try anything I thought could help Andrew. I was really just keeping busy waiting for "the call" from Dr. Donnelly.

THERAPY PET

According to a few of the books in my new autism library, autistic children naturally bond with animals. The reasoning is that it is not necessary to exchange words, since animals don't talk, and there are no social cues between owner and pet. Well, that was that. Andrew was getting his own pet. After much discussion, we were thinking something along the lines of a hamster, guinea pig, rabbit, something like that. We started our quest for the perfect pet early one morning. We were determined and in agreement that Andrew would be picking his own pet. After three pet stores, hundreds of choices, many trips to wash our hands, and tons of debate...Andrew got a puppy. A what? Yes, I know. I still have two kids in diapers. I know a fish would have been ideal. But he wanted a caramel-colored Pomeranian puppy. The puppies were in a corral on the floor in the third pet store we visited. Andrew walked in the door and ran for the puppies in the corral. He leaned over and tried to pick up our future pet. I asked him if that was the puppy he wanted to hold and he signed yes to me. He wouldn't put it down. Clutched to his chest he said, "Mine, puppy mine." So at the end of the day, the puppy was his.

Once at home, we thought it was important to name him. I tried to suggest names that one, Andrew could say, and two, were in his area of interest. I put out several of Andrew's toy trains, the ones I knew he could say the names of, and told him to pick one. Andrew picked Toby, a steam engine in the Thomas the Train series. That's how the puppy got his name.

The dog instinctively knew that he was Andrew's pet. Andrew and Toby were thick as thieves. Andrew seemed so happy, genuinely happy. I wasn't sure who the most beneficial recipient of the therapy pet was, maybe me. There were no words to describe how my heart felt, watching them play in the backyard. A boy and his dog: a mutual, unspoken, unconditional love and acceptance. Isn't that what we all want?

SUCKER

Rebecca, my loyal, candy-providing, child-entertaining, mobile haircutter, showed up once again for the fun. If you could have heard the drama in my back yard, you would have thought that Andrew was having a limb amputated without anesthesia. It was just a haircut. Yes, a hair cut. Picture this: he's sitting in the baby swing. Thomas the Train in one hand, a sucker in the other. He had Rebecca pulling out all the stops; singing, dancing, doing her best to work as fast as possible. He had both his sisters in on the act, crying with him. It was so ridiculous. I was confident that at least one of my neighbors was calling Child Protective Services as all of this was going on. I had a vision of the police knocking on my front door and me saying, "Officer, I know it doesn't sound like it, but my son is just having his hair cut. Oh, those girls crying? It's his sisters. That's sympathy crying. Yes, I agree, Officer, it is a strange phenomenon." All I kept thinking was: Is it happy hour yet? My blood pressure was so high I couldn't believe that my head didn't pop off my body. Rebecca has the patience of a saint, not to mention she works at Mach speed. My huge tip was a direct reflection of my strong desire for her to come back and do this all over again. I apologized profusely, she smiled politely. What I didn't understand was, in any circumstance where you would expect him to cry because you knew something hurt, you'd get no response from him. His doctor said it comes with the territory, having an extremely high tolerance to pain. But then we all know there is nothing painful about a haircut, yet it ignites a firestorm of drama. After all of this, I just want to know; where was *my* sucker? My behavior was certainly better than anyone else's today.

CALLED UP

We got the call. We were heading to California to see Dr. Donnelly. I felt like a minor league player who'd been waiting for their chance to play in the majors. Dr. Donnelly was in a league of his own when it came to specialists. I was nervous and excited at the same time. I knew that after this meeting there would be no need for further assessment. Dr. Donnelly was so well-regarded, it was understood that Andrew's truth would be revealed in this appointment, and I accepted that. I looked to this appointment with an unrealistic optimism. I knew on an emotional level, I wanted him to tell me that it wasn't true, that Andrew was not autistic, he was just delayed. I knew that on an intellectual level I was setting myself up for disappointment. My heart and brain were at war.

It was with a hopeful spirit that I headed to California, the Golden State, with Andrew, my golden boy. I was leading with my heart this time.

EVEN A DOUGHNUT COULDN'T FIX IT

We spent four hours with Dr. Donnelly. After our appointment, and as I was driving down the freeway, my head began to swim. I started to feel my chest tightening and my breathing getting shallow. I could feel my heart pounding in my eardrums, and my face was flushed with heat. I felt sick to my stomach, and my hands were shaking uncontrollably. I pulled off the freeway and right into a doughnut shop to find solace.

As I stared at Andrew across the table, my heart hurt. I mean, physically hurt. I watched him happily eating his doughnut holes, oblivious to the world around him. He didn't even notice that I was crying. I wasn't just crying, I was sobbing. My entire body was heaving as I was struggling to catch my breath. He didn't see me, even though he was looking right at me. My pain didn't even register to him, and up until that moment, I didn't even know this kind of pain existed. And so the two of us sat there all afternoon in the doughnut shop. Andrew in his world, and me in my personal abyss. Both of us oblivious to the world around us.

FINDING CENTER

With some time to digest, process and get some perspective, I write this entry with a heavy heart and hopeful spirit. Dr. Donnelly was all that I had hoped and expected him to be. He was an encyclopedia of knowledge, but in a practical and applicable way. He was so nice, kind and genuine. It took me no time at all to realize that he really does care about the kids that he takes on as patients. It isn't only the kids he cares about, but the families, too. He led me down the path of acceptance. He took time to address all the areas of delay and deficiencies in Andrew's development. I now had a better understanding of what autism is and what that means for Andrew. While I don't have to give up all my dreams for Andrew, I do need to embrace realistic expectations for him. This will take time. I choose not to see the problems, but to acknowledge that we have some opportunities for growth, both Andrew and myself. I tried my hardest to stay composed as I thanked Dr. Donnelly for everything. I finally cracked when I started to talk about my gratitude for his compassion. He grasped my hand and said, "This is not my quote, but you may find this helpful; sometimes life pushes us to the edge to help us find our center."

Wow, finding center. I'm going to start moon walking back from the edge and look for a more peaceful place in the center. That's my new survival strategy.

In a nutshell, the red wire does not connect with the red post. Andrew is just hardwired differently. He sees the world differently. There are several areas of concern for Andrew. His developmental delays are most evident in his lack of receptive and expressive language skills. Not far behind is his inability to communicate, impaired social interaction and restricted/repetitive behaviors, just to name a few. Now that I really understood what the problems were, I could focus my efforts better. I knew, based on what every professional I've seen has told me, that early intervention is critical. I asked Dr. Donnelly what he would do if Andrew were his son, and he pulled out a sheet of providers, circled a few, and handed it to me. He suggested a speech therapist at the Crimson Center in San Diego, and a specialized educational program designed to address the specific needs of children with autism, also in a suburb of San Diego. Before I left Dr. Donnelly's office, I knew that staying in Arizona was not in the best interest of Andrew. Among other things, the inability to access services alone would not get Andrew where he needed to go. Andrew deserved the best, and that was what he was going to get. San Diego, here we come!

SAN DIEGO OR BUST

Everyone agrees that, putting our family aside, there is nothing for Andrew in Arizona. It's hard to put the family aside. My mom and dad were here almost every day for their baby fix. The kids were really going to miss my dad, the "Egg Man." Who was going to make us breakfast every day? Quite honestly, that would be the hardest for me. I didn't know what I would do or how I would do it without them. It would be just the three little kids and me. I'd be a subsidized single parent. Tom was going to stay behind, since his law practice is there. His two older children would remain with him also. I couldn't speak for him, but I thought that staying behind was an easier choice for him both personally and professionally. I thought it'd been a long time since we'd brought out the best in each other, and I was sure that the distance would do us both some good. I was going to miss my friends and all the things that had become familiar to me over the last 18 years. I was sure my friends would come visit me in the summer when it was 115 degrees in Arizona, and 75 degrees in San Diego. Who doesn't want somewhere to go during the summer months? The little kids would miss their big kids, and vice versa. The reality was that I had to face myself every day and be able to say that I was doing the best I could for Andrew. I knew in my heart of hearts that this was what was best for Andrew. I knew that everyone that mattered to us believed that, too. We would all adjust. We had to. The heart wants what the heart wants, and my heart was with my quiet, little Andrew.

PRESCHOOL (AGE 3-4)
2006-2007

WHAT I DID ON MY SUMMER VACATION

I moved myself and three young kids from Arizona to San Diego that summer. We moved into a tri-level townhouse in a cute master-planned community. I logged a lot of miles going up and down two sets of stairs carrying Andrew and Sophia at the same time. We spent most of our summer going from therapy appointment to therapy appointment, with our schedule revolving around Andrew. I found a great pre-school program for Isabella with an early entry kindergarten curriculum to keep her challenged. Sophia would be old enough in January to go to the same school, so for now she'd tag along with me. We didn't have a television, by choice, and so we'd spend a lot of our time doing flashcards and playing games with each other. I bought each kid a disposable camera, and we had been taking pictures of familiar things to make picture books for Andrew to help improve his vocabulary. I thought that I'd have more visitors than I'd had, since San Diego is so beautiful. My mom had been coming over to help for at least ten days each month. I'd try to take care of all my errands, shopping and appointments for the time frame when I knew that I would have help. I was up for the challenge, but all the changes were a bit isolating. I was looking forward to getting the kids into school so that I would have an opportunity to meet new people. I thought the kids transitioned into their new life there very nicely. No major hiccups yet. Change is hard, but I thought everyone was up for the adventure.

THE RESULTS ARE IN

As a mother, it was really hard to sit and hear, really hear, about all the areas that Andrew is developmentally delayed. While there was an occasional surprise skill sprinkled in, the majority of the testing revealed some significant delays.

A typical child's expressive language skills develop in a progression from the use of gestures, to the use of gestural signals paired with speaking, and eventually, the use of verbal language. Gestures provide a bridge for a child as they move from non-verbal to verbal.

Andrew's gestural development score was twelve to fifteen months. He is thirty-four months old. He tested significantly below age level at this time. During testing, Andrew used a wide range of conventional gestures, but they did not coordinate with an eye gaze or physical touch. His gestures served more of a means to an end than an intentional communicative gesture.

Also, significantly below age level was Andrew's expressive (actual speaking) language skills. His score at fifteen months was a surprise to me. While I understood his delay, I thought we had made a tremendous amount of progress over the last three months. Guess I was wrong. Andrew used immediate echolalia (word or phrase repetition) for a variety of two-word utterances. He repeated words out of context, and used pronouns inappropriately. Not surprisingly, Andrew was able to label common objects. He also changed a word or words using mitigated echolalia. This was encouraging because it indicated that Andrew was beginning to understand the underlying rules of the English language.

The language comprehension score at eighteen months seemed low (which it was), but it was encouraging to me because it indicated he understood what was being said to him. It was an important precursor to the emergence of spoken language. Andrew was able to follow single-step directions, identify body parts, identify actions, and parts of a car. Andrew scored the highest in this area, which meant he understood more than he could acknowledge or appropriately respond to.

With a score of twelve to fifteen months, pragmatics or social communications skills were another area of deficit for Andrew. This area of communication referred to a child's ability to intentionally communicate. His ability to engage in intentional or goal-directed communication was noted to be an area of weakness, in the absence of high-affect. Andrew did not spontaneously initiate a request for assistance but instead, chose a new activity. He also did not spontaneously initiate communication for the purpose of social interaction. Andrew preferred to play alone, but was interested in what others were doing. He had difficulty taking turns and sharing.

This was a lot of information for me to take in and digest in one sitting. I was emotionally prepared for the worst, so there were really no big surprises. I left this meeting with specific recommendations for Andrew that the professionals had outlined for me:

1. Use the More Than Words program to support his communication development.

2. Intensive, individualized speech and language therapy.

3. Regular meetings between parents, educational staff, and therapeutic staff to ensure that treatment efforts and approaches are consistent.

4. A specialized educational program designed to address the specific needs of children with autism.

With these recommendations in place the goals for Andrew were as follows:

1. Increase the sophistication of his expressive communication skills to include a greater variety of conventional gestures, single words, developmentally appropriate word combinations, and simple sentences.

2. Increase Andrew's ability to communicate effectively across contexts and people (adults and peers) by directing his communicative signal with gaze and gestures and or words.

3. Demonstrate an increase in his rate of intentional communicative behaviors and increase his reciprocal exchanges to greater than four turns.

4. Increase his understanding of functional vocabulary, early linguistic concepts, and verbal directions across communicative partners and contexts.

5. Increase the sophistication of his play and imitation skills to include a variety of one-, two-, and multi-step play schemes based on familiar experiences.

It all sounded so overwhelming, but I knew that once I met with the pre-school intervention team, they could help break this down into a manageable plan. My wish for Andrew was that he could communicate his needs to me, and that I could feel like he understood me. I felt better in some ways that day knowing that he had the skills to learn, understand and use language. It was just going to take a lot of hard work to get him up to speed.

POSSIBILITIES

I met with the director of the pre-school program Andrew would be attending. They reviewed all of the testing, and developed an individualized education plan (also known as the IEP). I was so impressed with this school. I thought I ran a tight ship at home. I've got nothing on this place. The curriculum is highly specialized to fit the specific developmental challenges of each autistic child. For Andrew, there were core developmental challenges in the areas of communication and socialization that required some specific intervention efforts. The plan was to facilitate communicative intent and reciprocity, imitation, language use and comprehension, and play skills. What this really meant was helping him initiate and maintain a conversation, think of things to say, give him open-ended questions to ask to keep a conversation going. Andrew would work one-on-one, and within small groups, during the instructional portion of his day. A professional with specific expertise would work with Andrew in his primary area of deficit (or vulnerability, as they like to call it), which is his inability to appropriately establish and maintain two-way communication. His educational team would include therapists and teachers, as well as paraprofessional assistants with specific training in autism spectrum disorders. For the next two years, Monday through Thursday, both Andrew and his team of educators would be working hard to prepare him for a mainstream/typical kindergarten classroom. Cara, the school director, stressed the importance of setting expectations high for Andrew: that if I expected a lot from Andrew, he would deliver. She saw his potential for greatness, just like I did. I knew he was in great hands. I would sleep well that night. I knew that this move was worth all the sacrifices. The possibilities that this school had to offer will change who he can be.

THE BUS

Early Intervention Director, Cara: Do you want Andrew to be like the other kids?

Me: Of course.

Cara: The other kids ride the bus.

Me: Um, I think I'd like to drive him.

Cara: Why? There is an aide on the bus that uses the time to work on social skills and vocabulary building. It will be good for him.

Me: Maybe after he adjusts to the new school.

Cara: I think you're the one having trouble adjusting, not Andrew. All the kids ride the bus. Let him be like the other kids.

Me: Um...I'm just a little uneasy with the idea.

Cara: Own it! You're uneasy because you know the social stigma attached to riding the little bus. You know what people are thinking about you when it stops at your house and you know what people are thinking about your son, because you've thought it a million times. You can't help him unless you accept him. He won't be proud of who he is if you are embarrassed of who he is.

I was ashamed to admit she was right—all of it. Every last painful word of truth she spoke.

Our house was the first house Monday morning. I would be standing there proudly holding my son's hand. Andrew would be riding the bus.

INSIDE OUT

As Andrew and I stood outside waiting for the bus to arrive, we reviewed his vocabulary flashcards to pass the time. It kept us both distracted. We could hear the bus approaching before we could see it. Once it appeared over the hill, I pointed to it and said, "The bus."

Andrew began to say, "The bus, the bus!" His excitement was palpable, and he boarded the bus enthusiastically.

As the bus drove away, I felt a wave of sadness wash over me. I wasn't sad about sending him to school, because I knew he'd be attending a great program. From outside appearances, it would be hard for anyone to know how I really felt. On the inside, I ached. That day I had accepted my reality. I never thought that the little bus would be stopping right outside my house, picking up one of my kids, delivering him to a special education program. For all the days that I lived in denial, that day I couldn't.

Logically, I understood that this intensive program was necessary for Andrew. I realized that there were many skills that he needed to develop. But that day, in that moment, I had a heavy heart.

I hoped Andrew had a great day at school. I'd be proudly standing on the curb, anxiously awaiting his return home on the bus. I wished that my insides could feel the way I managed to make the outside appear.

STANDING AT THE GATE

I followed the bus to school today. I couldn't help myself. I wanted to see, and yet I didn't want to. Crazy, I know. The kids all emptied off the bus and onto the playground like little soldiers. I sat in my car and watched. I could still taste the stomach acid in my mouth from earlier in the day. I just felt sick and helpless watching my son wander aimlessly around the playground. He couldn't balance well enough to ride a bike or a scooter. He physically couldn't figure out how to peddle a Big Wheel. He couldn't catch a ball. All the things most boys love to do, he physically couldn't do it. I wondered if he'd ever have a friend? A playmate? A confidant? He seemed so lonely; or was I projecting my loneliness onto him? He couldn't miss something he'd never had, but I could. I could use a friend, a confidant. But really, who wants to hear about all of this? It was so depressing.

As they all filed into the classroom, I got out of my car to see if I could see into the classroom from the gate. As I clutched the chain link fence to peer into the classroom, I knew that going to the school that day was a mistake. I didn't see him like I saw the other kids. My heart said he didn't belong there. My head knew it was true, but my heart just didn't want to believe it.

HARD WORK

He's the hardest-working kid I know. He goes to school Monday through Thursday, where he is over-managed from the moment he gets there until the moment he leaves. On Monday and Wednesday, we go to Speech Therapy in the afternoon. On Tuesdays we go to a Social Skills group and on Thursdays, Occupational Therapy. On Fridays, I try to arrange a play date at the park. Saturdays is swim lessons. Sundays we are doing Horse Therapy. There was never a complaint from him. Never. He seemed to enjoy it all.

His sisters deserve the real award. They didn't resent him or even seem envious of all the time and energy spent on Andrew. They just seemed to understand. They were helpful and kind to him. They brought things to do in all the waiting rooms we sat in. They were even making friends with the siblings and parents of the other children. They knew his schedule better than I did. Sometimes at therapy the PTs would ask the girls to join in and they'd do it willingly, really participating wholeheartedly. Who are these kids, and where did they come from?

And me? I was just tired. Tired of all the driving. Tired from being "on" all the time. Tired of all the preparation to make sure we had everything. Tired of carrying two small kids up and down two sets of stairs day in and day out. How could I complain when my kids didn't? Emotionally, mentally, spiritually, physically exhausted: that's me.

HOPE

It's funny that the word *hope* can mean many different things. It can be a state of being. It can be a feeling. Hope can also be described as the act of looking forward to something desired. Hope can be a noun, a verb, a concept. In my case, hope came to me in the form of a person, Miss Hope.

Miss Hope was one of the teachers at Isabella's new pre-school. She introduced herself to me one morning when I looked particularly haggard. Miss Hope let me know that she does some babysitting outside of school if I ever need anyone, even just to run to the grocery store. I knew that any pre-school teacher was qualified to watch my kids. I just worried in particular about Andrew. She assured me she has experience with autistic kids, and even had one in her classroom that year. I was glad she was persistent. I finally made plans for her to come. Just for a quick outing. A trial run, so to speak.

Actually, I just wanted to go to Dairy Queen for a Blizzard without any kids. It took me more time to give Miss Hope the rundown on everyone than to get to DQ and back. The kids loved her, especially Andrew. It was nice because she has three boys of her own. I returned to a peaceful home, and a clean kitchen. Are you kidding me? A clean kitchen. I'm sold for that reason alone.

Leaving the kids with Miss Hope, gave me hope. Hope that I could get out to run errands, take the girls to activities, and take Andrew to therapy without the girls. Give our life some normalcy. While my idea of normal had certainly changed, I now had hope that we could make it all work. How synchronistic is it that my hope was named Miss Hope?

I LOVE YOU

Every day since the day Andrew was diagnosed, I worked on the sign for "I Love You." My girls instantly got it. It was what we did when I dropped them at school and picked them up. It was my way when we were at the park to engage with them. I'd sign "I Love You" and they'd sign back, and then I'd sign "I Love You More." Today the girls were playing tic-tac-toe with sidewalk chalk while we waited for Andrew's bus to drop him off after school. The bus pulled up and Andrew was in the front seat, watching us through the window. I gave him the sign and guess what? He signed "I Love You More" back to me. I could feel the knot in my throat. The girls started jumping and shouting, "He did it! He did it, Mom!"

He did it. Even if he never said it, I knew he loved me.

CRIMSON

We spent our summer and are now into fall, driving three days a week to the Crimson Center for speech therapy and occupational therapy. Worth the time, miles, and expense for more than one reason. First of all Karyn, the owner/director, is the one working directly with Andrew for his speech therapy. She doesn't care if he wears shoes, or doesn't; carries trains, or doesn't; brings his sisters, or doesn't...whatever it takes. Karyn was the first professional to tell me that Andrew has the ability to learn and understand language. That proclamation in and of itself was the greatest gift that I could have received. Just that knowledge alone made all the effort worth it.

Second of all, in such a short period of time, his vocabulary has really improved. It's not spontaneous language, but he knows a lot of words and can repeat many two-word phrases. I would love for him to just start talking to me one day and just give me an idea of what he's thinking about, but realistically, I think we are a long way away from that.

The third reason I didn't mind making the trip is Andrew's occupational therapist Kristina. She observed almost immediately that Andrew was intrinsically aware of his deficits, and would avoid those situations that challenged him beyond his capabilities. She could talk him into trying just about anything. He was easily frustrated, and his ability to imitate seemed limited. He couldn't catch a ball or toss it back. I just always took for granted that kids could catch and throw a ball. He would pick it up and walk it back. I thought it was fair to say that there was a noticeable discrepancy between Andrew's chronological age and his functional performance in gross motor skills. That being said, Kristina never gave up on him and could talk him through his frustration and tears. Breaks my heart to see him struggle.

While the color crimson represents love and blood, the Crimson Center has been a place where people who truly love what they do are giving Andrew their blood, sweat and tears. As his mother, I couldn't appreciate any more than I already do how much of themselves they gave to my son.

SUPPORT

Dr. Donnelly thought it would be a good idea if I tried going to a support group. I reluctantly agreed, but I supposed he had a good point. It might be nice to meet some other moms in the same situation. I might even make a friend, you never know. I wasted a lot of time figuring out what to wear. I should have just worn black. That night was more depressing than a funeral. Forget our kids; talk about a group of people that could use a social skills class. I went with a great attitude. I thought maybe I could learn a few things. Maybe I could get some good referrals. I might even find someone to have lunch with. What I found was my attitude for gratitude. I was thankful for the challenges I had. I had a woman ask me, "What's your kid's deal?"

I answered, "Well, he's autistic."

"Yeah, I got that," she said. "You know his deal—how does he stim?" (Stim or Stimming is shorthand for self-stimulation. It's a repetitive body movement, like spinning the wheels on something, hand-flapping, body-rocking, or head-banging, for example.) Who asks that? She said, "Trains, cars, what?"

I said, "Trains. Thomas the Train. I own every last one of them." By the way, after that night I thought my next letter should be to the company that manufactures Thomas the Train. I thought that the least this company could do would be to donate to some autism charity. Apparently every person there has every last train too, and every popular toy, T-shirt, movie and book. Putting this woman aside, no one else asked about my son. But I can tell you every last detail of every family there. Every last depressing detail. Driving home I decided, no more support groups for me. Next time I get a sitter, I'm going to Dairy Queen for a Blizzard; it will be more therapeutic.

PAVLOV

I had been asked by the director of the pre-school program to use the same incentive system at home that they used at school. I had no idea the power of the mini M&M. I was officially armed and dangerous, stocked up with a case of them from Costco.

We now had the same picture chart that they used at school hanging in our kitchen. The purpose of the chart was so that Andrew could see the order of activities, and once the activity was complete, he could exchange the picture card for an M&M. I worked carefully with his teacher to target specific at-home goals.

The three main goals we were focusing on were walking up the stairs without assistance, building vocabulary through flashcards and picture books, and using words when cued to ask for specific items. These were big goals that required a tremendous amount of patience. It was hard when Andrew was frustrated and crying for me not to just give him what he wanted without waiting for him to use his words. What was worse was when Isabella or Sophia would just say it for him. They couldn't help it, they just hated to see him cry. Me too, actually.

The easiest of the three goals seemed to be walking up the stairs without help. I stood on the landing above with the tube of M&Ms, holding it out where he could see it. It was actually really cute; he couldn't move fast enough to earn an M&M.

I never knew I was capable of so much patience. It was difficult not to just give in. I knew that if I didn't keep at it over and over, he would never progress. Some days I wasn't sure who was more trained: me in withholding the reward, or Andrew who knew what he needed to do to get it. Some days were a bit of a standoff, and some days, I would have liked to just let Andrew do what he wanted and I'd like to eat the M&Ms.

FEEDING FRENZY

If I hadn't been living it, feeding time would have actually been comical. Isabella must have a pink plate, pink fork and pink cup. Andrew must have the green plate, blue fork and cup with his name on it. Good thing baby Sophia was too little to get in on the action. For Isabella, none of the food could touch. If it wasn't soft food, Andrew wasn't eating it. He actually gagged and sometimes threw up. After reading the book about all the mercury in fish, I'd decided no more fish. I knew from Andrew's blood work that he didn't have any metals in his blood, but better safe than sorry. Although, I'm not sure how much worse it would be. So I substituted fish night for a new and exciting pizza night. This idea launched like a lead balloon. I was overly optimistic that if the food was presented in the normal fashion, that everyone would just eat it. Ha, joke was on me. I can certainly understand what drives a person to drink. Just try feeding my incredibly inflexible group of young eaters. Happy hour is on me!

OLD MCDONALD'S

I was unloading the dishwasher one day when the most amazing thing happened. Andrew appeared in the kitchen and tugged at my sleeve. When I turned to him he said, "I want French fries." I couldn't believe my ears. What? I just stared at him blankly. A smile began to spread on Andrew's face. He said it again, "I want French fries."

"Girls, girls, come downstairs!" I yelled. It sounded like a herd of elephants bounding down the stairs. As they approached the kitchen, I was holding Andrew proudly in my arms. "Tell the girls, Andrew," I said.

"I want French fries," he said. The girls started clapping and hopping up and down; his first request! Andrew's first true sentence. I told everyone to grab their shoes, we were going out for French fries.

On the drive to get fries, my eyes were full of tears. I could hardly believe it. Andrew had asked for something. In that moment my new motto was, "If he could ask for it, he could have it." Sitting at the stop light, waiting to turn in, Andrew said, "Old McDonald's, for French fries."

"That's right, we're going to Old McDonald's for French fries." There was no part of me that could tell him it's McDonalds, not Old McDonald's.

Sitting in the play area watching the kids eat their French fries, I was really overwhelmed by emotion. While it wasn't, "I love you" French fries at Old McDonald's felt just as good.

NEMO

"Two seconds is too long." That's the public service announcement that's on 24/7 regarding water safety. Since the day I got pregnant with Isabella, I had been crazy about water safety. We even filled in the pool at our last house before Isabella was born, that's how crazy I was. The strategy for swim lessons this year was: Sophia would go to childcare, and Andrew and Isabella would be in the same class. I talked it up to Andrew about how he would be swimming like Nemo in no time. I thought it would help having Isabella in class with him. You would never believe where I found my little Nemo a few days ago. I can only tell this story because it has a happy ending. Once lessons started, I decided to go back out to my car to get my soda that I had forgotten earlier. Instead, I stopped at the snack bar and just bought one. Walking back across the pool deck, I realized I couldn't see Andrew. Panic set in. I started running to the pool yelling at the instructor, "Where is Andrew? Where is Andrew?" By the time I got to the edge of the pool, I saw something that would haunt me forever. Andrew was at the bottom of the pool. Nothing, *nothing* prepares someone to see their child lifeless at the bottom of a pool. The lifeguard (who previously had been working on her suntan with her back to the pool) dove in, fished him out and began CPR. As he began to throw up everywhere, Isabella began to flip out. Nothing would ever compare to my subsequent flip out. The one place as a parent I had assumed (obviously incorrectly) that my kids were water safe, was in swim lessons. Note to self: don't take eyes off kids in water for any amount of time. Our pediatrician insisted that I get the kids back in the pool as soon as possible for my sake as well as theirs. The closest my little Nemo is getting to water in the near future is the bathtub, for my sake!

MOTHER/DAUGHTER BRUNCH

I felt bad for the girls that so much of our life revolved around Andrew's schedule. Not that anyone was complaining, I just felt guilty. I was actually blessed that they had never known anything else, because they just accepted that it is what it is. A mom in Isabella's kindergarten class hosted a mother/daughter brunch one day. Since her dad was in town and could watch Andrew and Sophia, Isabella and I left early so I could take her to get a mani-pedi. Talk about overcompensating! I think I was 18 before I had my first manicure. Honestly, it was worth every penny. She really enjoyed the time that she had me all to herself. Not to mention I let her pick out whatever color she wanted for her fingers and toes. (And yes, this did require extreme restraint on my part!) I really loved the mom that hosted the brunch. For the first time since we moved here, I really felt like I connected with someone. Her daughter has special needs. I really understood the motivation for brunch today. I was like this mom, in the sense that I felt like I had overcompensate when it came to other kids, in the hope that they would be nice to my kids. I wasn't sure that it really always worked, but I really did put in the effort. This mom was so gracious and kind. She talked all about what her daughter had been through, and all her hopes for her. I just felt the tears welling up when she spoke. I hoped that every mom there got her message, because it really was the same as mine: Use our children as an opportunity to teach your children about disabilities, about accepting others the way they are.

Our kids have challenges that most people probably won't ever understand, but people can teach their children to show compassion. When our kids have a temper tantrum, it's not because we are raising spoiled brats, it's because they can't communicate their frustration. Ask your children to treat our kids like they would want to be treated. Our kids need someone to eat lunch with and play with on the playground. Encourage your kids to do it. They aren't going to catch the disability. It's not communicable. Please don't judge us. We really are doing the best we can.

Walking to the car after the brunch, I asked Isabella if she had a good time. "Best day ever," she said.

"You know, her daughter is like Andrew," I said.

"I know, Mom, that's why her mom is so nice, just like you!"

HORSE SHOW

It's hard to believe that horse therapy turned out to be one of Andrew's favorite activities. It's hard to believe that at three years old, we started lessons for therapy, and not even a year later, he was competing in a horse show. His dad and all his grandparents arrived for the big horse show. We'd been talking about it for weeks now, since Andrew would be riding in a facility that he was not familiar with, and we all know how good with change he is. NOT!

When we got to the arena, I could see that this was not going to be an easy sell. Truth be told, I'm not sure how I got talked into letting Andrew compete anyway. My parents took the girls to go look at the horses. I tried to get Andrew to go with Miss Meg, his riding instructor, and owner of the stables where he rides. As Andrew started to cry, I began to wonder, how important is this? There was part of me that thought it was important to push him to do things, and then there was the softer side of me that thought all the drama just wasn't worth it.

It was time to get Andrew on his horse, Butterscotch, and get into the holding pattern for competition, and he was in hysterics. I could feel my blood pressure rising. I didn't know why, but finally I asked Miss Meg, "Is Hector here?" Hector is her ranch hand who doesn't speak any English, but he really seems to understand Andrew. Meg frantically began to call for him, and he came running. He swooped Andrew up into his arms. He began speaking in Spanish to him. I had never seen anything like it. Andrew stopped crying and got on the horse. Hector took the lead and got him into place for competition. We took our place in the stands and were amazed as Andrew came into the arena for competition without a tear on his face. He did it. I was so proud. Andrew placed third in his age bracket, quite an accomplishment for a beginning rider. He wouldn't accept his ribbon, because it wasn't the first place blue ribbon. I guess we probably need to work on sportsmanship, but I think I'll save that for another day.

STINK BOMB

My son officially has his own theme song: "Stink Bomb, Stink Bomb, Shoobie is a Stink Bomb." Man my kid stinks! I cannot get him potty trained fast enough. I have tried everything, and I am reasonably frustrated. I take him in every 15 minutes and ask him to just sit and do "good trying." Then I went to the more extreme route and tried tough love. No diaper or pull-up for 21 days, except at night (I'm not that crazy). I cannot tell you all the laundry and cleaning I did. I read several books looking for advice, and I finally realized that this is just one of those things that the autism impacts. When in doubt, I just relied on the wisdom of Dr. Donnelly, who informed me, "He just isn't ready." Clearly!! He did say that if Andrew wasn't potty trained by the time he was seven, he owed me a cup of coffee. Wa-wa-what? Seven? Four years from now? That is one free cup of coffee I hope I never collect on.

CAN I BRING A FLASK?

Andrew brought home an invitation to a classmate's birthday party. This was one brave mother. Beyond having family over, I had never had a party for Andrew. Number one: I didn't think he could handle the noise level and chaos of a large group of kids. Number two: and more important than number one, I'm not sure that *I* could handle the noise level and chaos of a group of autistic kids. I guess there was a part of me that could stay in denial, if I'm not hosting a group of Andrew's peers. I also thought I'd have to know my limitations. That's a lot of crazy, and I respect anyone that wants to do that for their kids. As long as Andrew isn't asking for a party, I'm not throwing one.

I was a nervous wreck, and the party was still a week away. I had played out every possible calamity to the Nth degree. I really wanted to ask the mom, beyond bringing my kids, can I bring my flask?

FLASK FOLLOW-UP

The party was at a local park with a bounce house. The good news is, Andrew spent most of the day in the bounce house. Isabella played on the play structure at the park, and I had my mom, who was visiting from Arizona, there to chase Sophia. Andrew did not understand that the gift we brought was for his friend. I know that this is hard for even typical kids. I had to promise Andrew he could have one if he could give the gift to his friend without any crying. Mission accomplished, and toy earned by Andrew. He didn't want to participate in eating lunch with his friends from school, or birthday cake, or even the opening of the gifts. Actually, that was a bit of a relief. Who knows what other toys I might have had to offer up. It was as if he was in his own world. Alone, in a room full of people.

I met a lot of moms today who were full of advice for me. I didn't ask for any, so it must have appeared as if I needed it. My mom said in the car after the party that all the moms (me included) had the same war-torn look on our faces. I guess the truth is, we are more alike than not. Some of us just carry nicer handbags. We all have the same heavy concerns, worries, doubts, and fears for our kids. We have a tired look about us that goes deeper than physical. It's emotional. It's mental. It's a constant nagging that never goes away. The daily responsibilities and weekend activities are just distractions from our truth. Once the parties are over, our daily duties done and the sun sets, the darkness creeps in. It creeps into our thoughts and our hearts.

What will become of Andrew? Who will take care of him if something happens to me? Who will understand him and love him like I do? This is why I dread the dark. The dark places of my head and my heart.

WHAT I LEARNED THIS YEAR

I had my end-of-the-year meeting to discuss any changes that needed to be made to Andrew's IEP for the fall. I was amazed at how many skills he'd mastered this year. I marveled at all the progress he had made this school year. Progress, not perfection; that's the mantra around my house. As a matter of fact, we had all learned a lot this year. For starters, I have the world's best mom. She would jump on a plane on a moment's notice and fly over to help. I couldn't ask for more than that.

I've learned that it's better to have one true friend than a handful of false ones. I am stronger and can do more on my own than I ever imagined. All the things I once thought were so important, really don't matter at all. Even if Andrew can never ride a bike, he is still going to have a happy childhood. I stopped judging others this year. We're all just doing the best we can. It's important to be nice, even when other people aren't.

My kids were learning by watching me and listening to me. They see and hear everything I do, even when I think no one is watching. I have to be the person I expect them to be. I accepted that I have a long journey ahead of me. I learned to focus and embrace all the things that make my kids special and unique. The things that bother me the most, will serve them the best in life. Most importantly, my son is still as perfect to me today as he was the day he was born. I'm not trying to change him. I want him to have the best life he can have, whatever that is for him. I love Andrew just the way he is.

As we wrapped up year one of Andrew's early intervention program, this was now what autism looked like to me: There are places in public that Andrew cannot handle because they are too loud. He can't see a movie in a movie theater and doesn't enjoy concerts. He has perfect pitch, so he can't stand to hear me sing. I always knew I couldn't carry a tune, but when your own kid covers his ears, you know it's true. The grocery store is sensory overload; the humming of the overhead lights, the smell of the food, the sound of the music, the visual complexities, all of it is way too much. Small changes in our routines are getting easier to handle. Big changes, big tantrums! Now that I am sensitive to it, I really notice the hand-flapping and the repeated walking in circles. I suppose that he has always done it, but now it's really obvious to me. He still loves Thomas the Train, but is starting to like the characters from *Cars*. While Andrew can't maintain a social conversation, he is learning the tools to start one. He has the ability to learn and understand language, which is a huge relief.

Much of his language was scripted, but I'm actually okay with that. His language was developing slowly, but he used it appropriately. He still preferred to play by himself and hadn't made any friends at school. He was learning strategies to look at people when they were talking to him, but continued to struggle with eye contact. He was beginning to play with his sisters, and seemed to be enjoying participating. Most autistic children have an area of excellence, and Andrew's is math.

While on many levels Andrew has made huge strides forward, in some ways he has stayed the same. I am fortunate that he was not aggressive. I am thankful that he didn't have tantrums at school. I would love it if he was potty trained, could dress himself, could brush his teeth, could use utensils when he ate, and could have a spontaneous conversation with me. Overall, I am thankful for all the positive things in our life. There is only one place to go, and that is up.

PRESCHOOL (AGE 4-5)
2007-2008

MILES TO GO

While I felt like I must have put fifty thousand miles on my car that summer, I still had a million miles to go in terms of getting Andrew where he needed to be. Andrew spent the first four weeks of summer enrolled in the extended school year program. I was thankful to have all the skills he had mastered being reinforced for an extra month. Andrew was definitely a "use it or lose it" kind of kid.

We spent our days driving to and from school, speech therapy, physical therapy, music therapy, art therapy, horse riding lessons, and trips to the beach...mommy therapy. I frequently questioned myself in terms of, am I pushing Andrew too much? I mean, whatever happened to the lazy days of summer? I wouldn't know. I was absolutely busier that summer than at any other time in my life. Some nights after everyone fell into bed, I wondered if I should just let Andrew play all day like other kids. Deep down, well, not even that deep, I knew that every professional he was working with would tell me to keep it up. In order for him to catch up developmentally, he had to be pushed. Even with all the effort, he may never catch up. He had made tremendous progress, but some days his skills slipped. Some days he was very withdrawn. I guess perspective is important; progress not perfection. So...we would just keep at it, one mile at a time.

THANK YOU

I was just sitting here thinking about all the things that I am grateful for. I think the biggest blessings in my life are all the people that work with Andrew. I wish that I could adequately express my appreciation to them, but I know that no gift is big enough, and I'd never be able to tell them without crying. If I could do it, this is what I would say:

Thank you for expecting excellence from my son and helping him to achieve it.

Thank you for treating him with genuine kindness day in and day out, especially when he is difficult.

Thank you for focusing on all the progress and positives.

Thank you for not caring when he wants to carry his trains and when he won't put his shoes on.

Thank you for never saying a word about the fact that he is still in diapers.

Thank you for showing up and giving your best, even on days when you don't feel like it.

Thank you for appreciating what makes Andrew special.

Thank you for accepting him for the way he is, and not trying to change him.

Thank you for making all the sacrifices worth it.

LIGHTENING MCQUEEN

After careful consideration, Andrew's birthday gift this year was a drive-able Lightening McQueen racecar. Are you kidding me? This is the cool-est thing ever. We took him to Toys R Us to pick out the car. He was like a baby chick, flapping his hands and hopping up and down. He looked like he was winding up for flight. Funny thing was, for the first time, I didn't care what people thought. He was so excited about this gift. Pure bliss. We got it out to the car and in the trunk. He wanted to sit in his car, while he was in my car. Best picture ever. It was all we could do to get him out of his car and into his car seat so that we could get home for him to take it for a test drive.

At home, he got behind the wheel and was ready to take it for a drive. The only problem was, he couldn't figure out how to keep his foot down on the gas pedal. This was the one thing we hadn't thought of; he didn't have the motor skills for the gift. Never fear, his sisters to the rescue. They took turns with Andrew as their passenger, driving him around the streets of our neighborhood. Andrew was just as happy to be the passenger, and he didn't seem to care that he couldn't figure out how to drive. It was my heart that was hurting for him. The girls got a new sports car that day. Good thing for the birthday boy he'd always have two drivers. Looks like he's going to need them.

THE HAPPIEST PLACE ON EARTH

Brave or stupid, I'll let you be the judge of that. I heard from one of the other moms that Disneyland offers a disability pass for kids with autism, so that you don't have to wait in line for the rides. What? No lines? Count me in. I took the kids to Disneyland. I enlisted the biggest kid I know to help, my sister, Auntie Lisa. We met at the front gate the minute the Magic Kingdom opened. I headed straight to city hall with Andrew's diagnostic paperwork in hand to get my hands on the disability pass. Guess what? I didn't even need the paperwork. They took my word for it. I guess now that I think about it, who would lie about their kid having a disability just to get a pass so that you don't have to wait in line at Disneyland? HMMMM, that was not a rhetorical question.

Best day ever. We blew to the front of the line on all the kiddie rides. You could hear people wondering who we were. They thought we had to be someone famous because we didn't have to wait in the line. Who knew having a disabled kid would give them rock star status at Disneyland? I am officially the biggest fan ever of Disney. We rode all the rides that the kids were big enough for, we ate all the junk we could stuff into our tummies, we got mouse ears, and other souvenirs. For me, I got a day where my son could just be a kid. He did it. He did the noise, he did the crowds, he managed the motion of the rides and he managed his emotions. We truly had the best day ever at the happiest place on earth.

THE DENTIST

I was dreading today for Andrew. He needed a lot of dental work, and in order for the dentist to work in his mouth, we agreed that sedation would be the best. In order to sedate someone so young, he needed blood work and an EKG, because of his earlier heart problems. After jumping through all those hoops, the insurance company refused to cover the sedation. Are you kidding me? The person making the decisions over there clearly had no idea what it was like to take an autistic child to the dentist, let alone try to fill cavities and seal teeth.

I can tell you, after just getting him through the door of the office that day, I'm the one that could have used the sedation. I made the mistake of holding Andrew in my arms while they administered the anesthesia. Worst idea ever. I will never shake the image I have of his eyes rolling back into his head. I had this deep feeling of sadness as I handed him over to the anesthesiologist.

I walked slowly out to the waiting area where I was instructed to sit. It was just me and another mom. She had her head buried in her newspaper, which was fine with me. Who was really in the mood to talk, anyway? About ten minutes later the door to the waiting area opened and in walked a man carrying two cups of coffee, one for himself and one for his wife.

She looked shocked, and after she took her first sip she said, "How did you know how I like it?"

Husband replied, "I've watched you fix it every day for over ten years now." I pulled my magazine up to cover my face and started to cry. I was so alone. I would give anything for someone to bring me a cup of coffee. That's it, just a cup of coffee.

WILL I EVER?

Andrew came with me to pick up Isabella from kindergarten. I call it "Why Bother Wednesday?" The kindergartners have early release. By the time you drop them off and get home, it's time to go back and get them. Hence the "Why Bother Wednesday."

As we stood at the fence watching the kids play on the playground, Andrew was tugging at my hand. "Mommy, will I ever go to a normal school?"

I could barely choke out an, "I don't know, son." I had dreaded this moment for a long time. He did get it. He understood. It was painful. He wanted to know if he would ever, and I just didn't know. I just don't have all the answers. I imagined that we would have this conversation many times. The reality was, no matter how much work he put in, I put in, that's the million-dollar question. Will he ever?

BUTTERSCOTCH

Sunday, our favorite day of the week. We love packing lunch and going to Miss Meg's for Andrew's riding lesson. At riding lessons today, disaster struck. The girls and I were over petting the bunnies when we heard the screaming, both from Andrew and Miss Meg. I didn't even wait for the girls, I just started running for the corral. Andrew was thrown from the horse with such force that his helmet split open upon impact. This was Andrew's second fall in the past few weeks.

We originally started horse riding lessons for therapy, but Miss Meg said he was a natural horseman, so by the third week of lessons he was learning dressage. Actually, Andrew is a really good horseman. He has a natural connection with his horse, Butterscotch. Some days we stopped by just to bring Butterscotch carrots. I knew in my heart that we had to stop riding before Andrew got seriously injured. I understood when I signed him up for lessons that accidents happen, but I couldn't risk that he may have a life-altering injury, especially when we were making so many strides in other areas. After seeing his helmet, or what was left of it, I knew that this could have been so much more serious. So it was with a lot of sadness and tears that we said goodbye to Butterscotch that day. This was going to be so hard; he loved it so much. I had to carry Andrew to the car. What I really needed was someone to carry me.

THE GREEN APRON

After much thought and consideration, we decided I'd have to go back to work. I found a Starbucks that was happy to have me back and close to home, although not my neighborhood store. I was planning to work the closing shift from 6 to 11, Monday through Thursday. When my kids were just babies I used to work at Starbucks in Arizona. I worked the 3:45 a.m. to 8:00 a.m. shift. A logistical challenge for sure.

One of the teachers from Isabella's pre-school, Miss Kim, needed a place to live, so I offered her a room in my home, in exchange for watching the kids while I was at work. It was a win-win. I only had to work 20 hours a week for medical benefits, and that was what we really needed. Starbucks has truly exceptional medical benefits for employees and their families, covering even autism-related medical and therapy needs. It is an amazing company, and so caring of its personnel. Andrew's medical expenses were astronomical, and this was really the only way to make it all work. Every quarter, our medical insurance premiums were rising because of our usage, and many of Andrew's expenses weren't covered. Andrew got some benefits through Regional Center, but medical insurance was still our biggest expense. Regional Center was established by the State of California to provide services to individuals with intellectual disabilities. Regional Center provided Andrew with some speech therapy, some occupational and physical therapy, and also respite care.

The kids were really looking forward to Miss Kim moving in, and I was, too. It would be nice to have some adult company and an extra set of hands to help out. The kids really weren't going to miss me the last couple of hours of their day. That was really just bath time, TV or movie time and a quick story. I knew that they were going to be in good hands. This was going to be good for me, too. It would be good for me to talk to adults and get out of the routine. I was actually looking forward to it. Looking forward to wearing the green apron.

MONKEY ON HIS BACK

There's a monkey on his back. Yes, I know. Andrew officially had to wear the monkey backpack. It was really a child harness disguised as a monkey backpack. Andrew had started opening the door of the car when we got somewhere, taking off his seat belt, and running through the parking lot. Not a joke. Instead of waiting for my kid to be hit and killed by a car, he now has the privilege of wearing the monkey.

This running in parking lot business was enough to drive me to drink. Not that there weren't a few other motivators on the table already. So... the kiddie leash it is. Safe kid: yes. Parental judgment: yes. Do I care about the judgment? Yes and no. Just a trip around the block in my shoes and I doubt I'd even get a sideways glance. I'd probably get sponsored for an adult beverage.

The reality is, I don't want my kid hit by a car and either seriously injured or killed. Do I want to put him on a leash to go out in public? No. Do I want him to see his next birthday and the one after that? Yes. That is why he will have a monkey on his back until he can use better judgment; on that day, there will be one less monkey on my back!

JUST A TRIM

Our favorite stylist left San Diego. After asking the other moms, I found someone who would be willing to cut Andrew's hair, all of them, in a salon no less. Interestingly enough, this girl has a special needs brother, so she has a place in her heart for special kids who do need haircuts from time to time. All of the moms used Amanda and loved her. They referred to her as the haircut whisperer. Game on! I made an appointment for all the kids and was talking it up the whole drive over. I was trying to sell the program, as we were all going to watch Sophia have her first haircut. If there was time...maybe Andrew could get just a trim. There was nothing but silence coming from Andrew's side of the car. Isabella talked the whole way there about how she wanted a haircut too. It was only a matter of time before they all outsmarted me, but I was pretty proud of myself for making it sound like there was only going to be time for Sophia today.

Thanks Econ 101: Supply and Demand at its finest. After introductions, Sophia climbed up into the chair. I took pictures, fussed non-stop about what a big girl she was, went on and on about how brave she was. When she was done, Amanda made a huge deal about her getting to pick out a sucker because she didn't cry. She invited Andrew over to pick out a sucker. She then went on to explain that his sucker had to sit in a special spot on her counter until the haircut was over. If there were no tears, he could have the sucker. If he cried, the sucker would go back in the container for another kid.

Genius! Why hadn't I thought of this? The sucker AFTER. Andrew climbed into the chair and she turned him so he could see his sucker and watch himself in the mirror. The haircut was off to a great start. On went the clippers and out of Andrews mouth came the highest pitched noise I have ever heard. It wasn't a cry. It wasn't a scream. It was other-worldly. Off went the clippers. Amanda finished up with the shears.

Andrew got the lollipop he had earned. He hopped down and ran over to sit by Sophia and eat his sucker. As he was unwrapping his sucker, I saw the corners of his lips curl into a smile. Pride. He was proud of himself. He did it. He'd earned it. On the drive home I praised all three of them up and down. What a great day. Another first; three haircuts and no crying from anyone, not even Mom.

NORMAL?

The program that Andrew was in had what they called "community kids" in the classroom. These were kids that were developing by age-appropriate standards (normal, whatever that is). So this school year, Sophia would be joining Andrew in his pre-school program as a "community kid" Monday through Thursday. This was nice for me, one-stop shopping, so to speak. I thought it was good for both Andrew and Sophia. On Fridays this year I had found a typical (normal) pre-school program that would take both kids. I had been encouraged to do this to see how Andrew does without one-to-one instruction. Sink or swim time.

Sophia is such a caregiver, I wondered how she would do. I was curious to find out if she would model the behavior and the tasks, or if she was going to try to take care of the kids and do it for them. I was willing to bet she'd be trying to do everything for everyone. We would see. I didn't try to potty train Sophia because I didn't want her to pass by Andrew. I was so consumed with how he would feel if she potty trained before him. Well, she potty trained herself, and Andrew was her biggest cheerleader. So much for my theories!!

There were certain things that I just assumed would bother Andrew, and what I was learning was that I can't think for him. Everyone is different, and each person sees each situation in a unique way. He genuinely was proud of Sophia for using the bathroom, with not a single thought of how it might reflect his development. Just writing this makes me seem ridiculous for expecting his thought process to be sophisticated enough to get that. Well, this should be an interesting year for the kids and for myself.

MY HOLIDAY WISH

This holiday season the only outing that I really wanted to do as a family was to go see the tree display at the Four Seasons. In an effort to set up the day for success, I had taken the kids to get a treat of Andrew's choosing. The girls were happy to go see the trees, so it was really only Andrew that I had to try to get on board with the program. I had been talking up this outing for days because I was so desperate for it to be a success, for the girls, for myself, and as a family.

The drive to the hotel itself was fine. Entering the hotel, I knew we were in trouble. I wasn't sure where I went wrong. I don't know if I waited until too late in the day and he was just too tired, or if it was the sounds of the music and the crowd combined with the lights and the smells. Andrew was on sensory overload, and the fast track to a major meltdown. I tried to divert him with some hot cocoa and a treat, but it didn't work. I tried carrying him, and he wanted no part of it. I couldn't even interest him in the train that was winding through an amazing gingerbread display.

He covered his ears and began to rock back and forth. When I picked him up, he started in with the high-pitched screaming. I couldn't get out of there fast enough. As we were driving home, I felt defeated and depressed. It was the only thing I had wanted to go out and do all holiday season.

The next day while we were at Andrew's appointment with Dr. Donnelly, I mentioned our failed outing. Dr. Donnelly suggested in the future, I get a sitter and take the girls. He said Andrew wasn't going to feel bad that I didn't take him because he really didn't want to go. He wasn't missing anything. Dr. Donnelly was right, he wasn't missing anything. It was me that didn't want him to be left out. I guessed I'd have to change how I felt about it. The girls and I were entitled to enjoy a holiday outing. It didn't make it any less of a memory if Andrew didn't come along. If he couldn't do it, he couldn't do it. But it didn't mean that the girls shouldn't get the chance to do it.

I wasn't sure why I needed a professional to tell me that it was okay to get a sitter and leave Andrew at home. I think deep down I really knew this already. Sometimes we just need someone to validate our decision or state the obvious. In my case, it was Dr. Donnelly.

A MOTHER'S WORST NIGHTMARE

At three o'clock the bus didn't come. By three thirty I was on the phone with the school. At four o'clock I was frantic and by four thirty, I had called the police. Andrew had fallen asleep on the bus and the substitute driver had dropped off all the kids and returned the bus to the district lot. He didn't notice that Andrew was still on the bus. By four forty-five I was certifiably crazy and by 5:00 p.m., when a district official dropped Andrew off, I was in the middle of a nervous breakdown. The police advised me to take Andrew to the emergency room for an exam.

This is your worst nightmare. A kid that has no spontaneous language, who couldn't tell me what happened, even if something did. Andrew is every predator's dream and it makes me sick, physically ill, to imagine that as one possibility. You know, you think that you are doing all you can to protect your kids, and then something like this happens. Well, I can tell you this; I may want Andrew to be like all the other kids, but he is never going to ride the bus again. NEVER!! I will say this; the emergency room doctors handled Andrew so nicely. They handled the police even better. They said since Andrew has echolalia (involuntary repetition of words spoken by another person) it was important to do a physical exam without asking questions, because they didn't want to provide him with something to repeat that had never happened. Genius! If you had told me that this was all going to end well I never would have believed you. While I was living this nightmare, my imagination had gotten the best of me.

HAPPY BIRTHDAY…AGAIN

I took the kids to Las Olas restaurant to celebrate my birthday. The kids did a really great job. I have no complaints. Plus, I got to have my nachos. After I put everyone to bed that evening, Andrew came in and asked if he could get in bed with me. This was a first, so I let him climb in. I was reading a book and he started to make this weird, clucking noise. I turned over and Andrew was having a grand mal seizure. I called 9-1-1, and by the time the paramedics arrived he was unconscious. As they were running an IV line and putting an oxygen mask on him I lost my nachos, everywhere. A few days in the hospital, lots of tests, one tired kid and one exhausted mom. My birthday gift this year? It's epilepsy, because life wasn't hard enough for Andrew.

MRI

Andrew needed an MRI. This was not an event I was looking forward to. I could think of a lot of other ways I'd like to spend ten grand; for example, on my own MRI: Moms Retail-therapy Investment. Anyway, it is what it is. Chalk it up to the cost of doing business. It really wasn't about the money, it was about the fear. Fear of, what are they going to find? Is it a tumor? Is it cancer? I had this constant, underlying fear that they would find a structural defect. It was a nagging fear, like a dull headache that the Advil couldn't take care of.

I sometimes wondered, what if Andrew really isn't autistic? What if it's a brain tumor? Both Dr. Donnelly and our pediatrician assured me that my abnormal fear was, well, actually quite normal. They both said that if I wasn't fearful, *that* would be abnormal. Hmmm, normal in the abnormal, or abnormally normal. Well, at least I had some time to adjust and get used to the idea. Or maybe just more time to worry. Either way, once the MRI was done, the questions would be answered. For me, the fear is going into the unknown, not knowing.

HEARTACHE

The last few days, my heart had been hurting. Over the last couple of years this has happened. I just wrote it off as anxiety over all the stuff going on. Tonight my heart started to hurt again, only this time I broke out in a cold sweat. Next thing I knew, I was in the back of an ambulance. I really don't remember anything, but according to my co-workers, I complained about my heart hurting and the next minute, I was on the floor. I passed out behind the counter at Starbucks. The paramedic told me they thought I was having a heart attack. What?

Well, lots of tests and hours later, I am pleased to say, I did not have a heart attack. According to my new cardiologist, who invited me to start running with him, my heart hurts because it is a muscle, and I am over exercising it. Who knew all that spinning wasn't so good for me? Not to mention, he doesn't think all the stress of raising three kids, one with special needs, on my own, is doing my heart any good, or my mental health. Which is why I love spinning. I love the cadence. The loud music. I just get lost for an hour and forget about everything. My spinning days are officially over for 30 days. So, the moral of the story, when I kept complaining that my heart hurt, it did. My heart isn't broken, it just hurts.

SPECIAL DAY CLASS

After two long years and lots of hard work, placement day has arrived.

Drum roll please.................

Andrew would be in the special day class for kindergarten at our home elementary school. After two years and hours of hard work, this was a huge accomplishment for him. Next year would be pivotal for him. He would spend part of his day in the Special-ed classroom, with the inclusion opportunity for all the areas he needs additional growth. For the areas in which he excels, he would join a typical, mainstream kindergarten classroom with an aide.

I was nervous for Andrew for this next year. It was crunch time. If he wasn't successful in this program, it would be off to a different school next fall. I was scared for him to be on the playground with typical kids. I wasn't sure how well he could navigate.

There are miles to go, but in the meantime, baby steps. First step, get him out of diapers before fall. There's nothing like a kindergartner in diapers to set him apart from his peers. I was worried about how this would be for Isabella. I wondered if the kids would tease her or make fun of her because she has a brother in the Special-ed classroom. Kids are mean. And if mean kids have mean parents, it's even worse. When parents look on while their kid says mean things, I secretly want to shout at them, "This could have happened to you, you know?"

Time to cross our fingers and hope for the best. We all could not have worked any harder to prepare him for this opportunity. I think Andrew has experienced tremendous growth this year. He was responding to his name and nicknames, most impressively when being called by someone other than myself. He was showing the ability to identify basic emotions in himself and others. While Andrew was attached to me and his sisters, at times he could appear disconnected. Almost all social cues are lost on Andrew. I was still hanging, waiting for the high five I asked him for this morning. I could extend my arms for a hug and he would walk right past me. The girls think it's funny and run into my outstretched arms, I suppose so I don't look so silly.

I thought that his inability to understand body language was presenting the majority of his social challenges. His language was extremely scripted, almost monologue-like. He had an unusually large vocabulary, I think they call it little professor syndrome, but can't seem to sustain a conversation. Good thing for Andrew that his sisters and I like to talk a lot, especially Isabella. When I can get her to close her mouth at night she falls asleep instantly. His repetitive behaviors have largely remained the same. He still flaps his hands like he's trying to fly, and he still liked to move in circles. He had started to place his trains in a very precise order. Good thing Isabella has a mind like a steel trap. She knew the exact order in the event it accidentally got screwed up when he wasn't home.

This school year I learned that GI issues affect a large number of autistic children. Apparently I don't have the only stink bomb out there. While we gave the wheat free/gluten free, casein free diet the good old college try, it didn't seem to have an impact either way. So we abandoned that ship. The other big correlation is seizure disorders and autism. While this was not on my short list of things that I was optimistic about, it was one of our biggest challenges this year.

While I was so entrenched in the day-to-day routines of raising three kids, I'd forget about all the progress we'd made. Some days were harder than others but overall, I couldn't ask for more from Andrew. He was the hardest working kid I know. All his hard work had really paid off, and I expected great things from him. He could do it. I knew he could.

IT'S A WRAP

As we wrapped up another school year, it looked as if it was a wrap on my marriage as well. Every-weekend visits, turned into twice a month, that turned into once a month, that turned into holidays only. It was inevitable. Perhaps even ordained.

To our credit, ours had been a civil divorce. Not an easy accomplishment in this day and age. Isabella, Andrew and Sophia had the good fortune of having been born to a man who, beyond being a loving, intelligent, ivy-league educated father, possesses a fine and good immediate and extended family. For Andrew especially, that is a very good thing.

I have three great children from my ex. For that reason alone he deserves my kindness and respect. I want my kids to have the best relationship they can have with him, and I will do everything in my control to help facilitate that. I know that just like me, he is doing the best he can.

KINDERGARTEN (AGE 5-6)
2008-2009

OPEN HOUSE

I took Andrew to meet his kindergarten teacher and special-ed class-mates today. I couldn't remember a single detail of the classroom or one word that the teacher had to say, but I can remember each and every kid in that classroom. My heart was beating so hard I could feel that familiar whooshing sound in my ears. By the time I hit the parking lot, I had started crying. For the first time since the day he was diagnosed, I finally said out loud how I really felt.

It wasn't fair. It wasn't fair that my only son is autistic. It wasn't fair that he had to be in a special-ed classroom. I just didn't see him like I saw those other kids. But he is. He is just like them. It just seems like a big mistake, like some big misunderstanding. Isn't it possible he is just a little delayed? I just wished he was going into a typical kindergarten classroom. My quirky little kid. I hated that he had to work so hard all the time and couldn't just enjoy being a kid. I hated spending day in and day out schlepping him from one therapy to the next, micro-managing every second of every day. I hated being "on" all the time. I hated try-ing to make everything a positive, an opportunity for growth. I hadn't stopped crying all day. I was a certifiable hot mess. Good thing I had a sitter, because for the first time in two years, I did exactly what I felt like doing on most days. I climbed into bed, pulled the covers over my head and cried, and cried, and cried.

BABY STEPS

Whoever coined the phrase "two steps forward, one step back," was definitely raising an autistic child. What I really want to know is, while they were taking all these steps, was their kid wearing shoes? Because, I can tell you, mine is not.

MY SPECIAL SECRET

For the past few weeks, after my kids were asleep (and with a babysitter), I'd been dating someone. I felt like a high school girl. He is tall, handsome, funny, and last but not least, a true gentleman. He is a nationally renowned trial attorney here in San Diego. I know, I know, not another attorney. But really, as he jokingly warned me from almost the first time we spoke, he "is not like other attorneys." He is so kind and such a good listener. Even when we are sitting in silence, I feel that he really understands me. Almost an unspoken understanding.

We have great banter. He cracks me up. Steve always takes me nice places and always shows me a good time, as he is apt to remind me from time to time. He has been pestering me for a while to meet the kids, but truth be told, I wanted to make sure that the relationship was going to last before I'd let the kids meet him. I thought that he would be meeting the kids sooner rather than later. I truly felt like I had met my soul mate. He seemed to treasure all the things that make me unique. Steve brought a tremendous amount of happiness and joy into my life. He even sang to me, my own special songbird. I honestly believed that he loved me because of it all, not in spite of it all. That says more about what kind of person Steve is than anything I could put into words.

TACO TUESDAY

After much deliberation, I decided to introduce Steve to my kids. I have a philosophy that if I'm not planning to keep a romantic someone in my life, then I'm not going to introduce him to the kids. That way, the kids only meet people I plan to have a meaningful relationship with. I told the kids we were going out for Taco Tuesday to work on our table manners. The kids had no idea that I had been dating Steve for months now, or that Steve was planning on meeting us there.

We sat down, ordered our dinner and were busy coloring when Steve arrived at our table. I introduced "my friend" Steve to the kids, and invited him to join us for dinner. He sat down between Andrew and Sophia. Isabella said, "Boy, you're tall, Steve." Andrew said, "Steve, I like your tie." We were off and running. Dinner went smoothly, and the kids did an amazing job. Sophia was sitting on his lap in no time flat. The girls colored pictures for him. Everyone seemed genuinely happy to have him there. He walked us to our car, after which we all said our good-byes, and went our separate ways. The kids didn't say a word about Steve the whole way home. I thought Taco Tuesday was a success.

UNEXPECTED KINDNESS

I worked with a young woman whom I treated like the little sister that I never had. Her parents really seemed to appreciate the advice and guidance that I'd been giving their daughter, and they invited all the kids and myself over for dinner. I was extremely nervous. Being a big group, we don't visit; we invade. The whole drive over I was busy giving the manners talk, the behavior talk. The entire drive was me regurgitating the Emily Post etiquette book.

I was exhausted by the time we pulled into their driveway. Their dog greeted us at the front door. The girls ran in and Andrew hid behind me. I think all of the excitement was overwhelming. I just picked him up and held on. I knew her parents already knew all there was to know about Andrew, so I was proud of the fact that I kept my mouth shut and didn't feel the need to explain away his behavior. I was trying a new approach.

We weren't there ten minutes and Andrew climbed down and began searching for their kitty with the girls. Dinner went seamlessly, and then the real fun began. Out came the karaoke machine. All the kids, Andrew included, were singing Christmas carols. Who knew? Her dad offered to follow us to the Christmas tree lot and help us get a tree and get it set up at home for me.

Off we went. In land speed record time, we had picked out a tree and were back at our house setting it up. When they were all leaving, I asked the kids to come and say good-bye. I can barely even see through my tears to write this. Andrew went up to her dad and hugged him and said, "Thanks for the best night, EVER." I believed him. I thought it was his best night ever. He participated from start to finish. The pure warmth and kindness of virtual strangers to Andrew brought out the absolute best in him. Just as they appreciated the kindness I had shown their daughter, I appreciated the kindness they'd bestowed on the kids and me.

WINTER GAMES

It was that time of year again, the annual trip to Coronado to go ice skating. This year, my overly ambitious parents wanted to take all three kids ice skating AND stay overnight at the hotel. Best part, they all wanted to go, even Andrew. What was I going to do with an entire night off? The possibilities seemed endless. I got everyone packed and thought it would be much better if I drove everyone to the hotel and got everyone settled. Once I thought everyone had acclimated, we headed out to the skating rink.

Andrew decided upon arrival that he actually didn't want to ice skate. Who can blame him, considering under normal circumstances his balance isn't that good? No worries, Papa took him for ice cream and into the hotel to admire all the Christmas decorations. The girls loved the ice skating. Mama took turns guiding them around the rink. It was such a beautiful day to skate outdoors; sun shining, palm trees swaying in the wind. An ice skating rink right on the beach, the setting seemed surreal. Watching the girls go around and around the rink with my Mom, I was overwhelmed with gratitude for my parents. In spite of everything with Andrew, they did their best to help all the kids have the most idyllic childhood possible.

After skating, I got everyone changed and ready for a big night with Mama and Papa. I myself had big dinner plans. Steve and I were planning to eat downtown, just in case I needed to drive over to Coronado to bring anyone (Andrew) back home with me. After dinner, I called my parents to check in and everything was going great, so I just headed home.

About one o'clock in the morning my cell phone rang. It was my dad. He was outside my front door with Andrew. Andrew had woken up and was inconsolable, so my dad drove him home. I don't know why my dad didn't call me, I would've gone and picked him up. I just appreciated that everyone gave it a try. Progress, not perfection. Andrew walked straight past me and walked right upstairs and climbed right into his bed.

In the morning I took Andrew out for breakfast, just the two of us. The girls had their grandparents all to themselves. I was just happy that last night I'd had dinner out and didn't have to cut anyone's food, or take anyone to the bathroom besides myself. Everyone was happy. I was learning that sometimes we can't all enjoy the same activity together, and that's okay. If Andrew doesn't feel like he's missing out on something, then who am I to miss it for him? Easy to say, hard to believe.

FAMILY MEETING

I called a family meeting. All the kids came running down to the family room. After everyone sat down in the circle I said, "I have a big announcement to make. The stork is coming. It's going to be bringing us a new baby." The kids went nuts. They were jumping up and down and clapping. I cannot put into words how happy the kids were. Andrew announced that he was hoping that the stork would bring him a baby brother. I dropped the bomb that the stork was actually bringing us a baby sister. Andrew said, "Oh, that's okay, Mom. Maybe Santa can bring me the baby brother." Maybe, not likely, but maybe. I just couldn't bring myself to tell him there was never going to be a baby brother. I'd save that disappointment for later. I hated to kill all that enthusiasm. It was funny, I'd worried the most about telling Isabella, and yet she seemed to be the happiest. Maybe because she was actually old enough to be able to help with the baby. Who knows? I guess you never really know how someone else will respond. Tonight's family meeting was a huge success. The kids cannot wait for the stork's arrival.

TESTING

Andrew needed some medical tests. He had an arm movement that looked like he was being electrocuted. Out of nowhere, his right arm would shoot up into the air, while his mouth pulled to the side in a grimace. The best way to explain it is to say it looked like he was being electrocuted, because his arm shot up with such velocity. He had been doing it for a while, and there was some concern that the medicine he took to control his seizures wasn't working.

I'd decided to take a leave of absence from work so that I could take Andrew to have the testing. It required an extended hospital stay, so I would need to make arrangements for the girls. Since it wasn't clear what the results of the testing would be, the next step was vague. I'm better in stages, anyway. The unknown is what makes me worry, but I am always good once I can make a plan. On the outside I am very low key and matter-of-fact.

The kids really seem to feed off me emotionally, so I have learned over time to lay low. I phrase everything in the positive, because I think perspective is so important. They look to me and at me to see what is really beneath the surface. I owe it to them to be a constant, positive role model. Knowing what is wrong is better, but the reality is such that it doesn't make a difference. It is what it is. I wish I could remember that when I'm lying awake at night, unable to sleep from all the worry. I guess that's my test; I hope I pass.

BEST PATIENT EVER

We checked in for Andrew's EEG. It took 45 minutes to glue all the electrodes into place and get him all hooked up to the machines. He was a trooper. He didn't cry or complain once. Not even a complaint about the smell of the glue. Unbelievable. This kid really has patience. I don't know where it comes from. We could all take a page out of his book.

He spent most of his day watching movies. Andrew tried some video games, but didn't really have the motor skills to enjoy playing, which was fine with me. The best part of his day was when the therapy dog came to visit. The dog had his own trading card, like a baseball player. The dog's owner let the dog climb in bed with Andrew; he loved it. He had a hamburger for lunch and dinner. Andrew was in heaven. Dr. Donnelly stopped by to let me know that the results thus far were abnormal, which he suspected that they would be, and was hoping to know more by tomorrow. At least I knew for sure that we were doing what we could to find some answers. Andrew was in the best care possible. I was sure that after the stressful morning we'd had, we would both sleep well that night, even if it was in a hospital bed.

CUP OF COFFEE

While reading in the hospital bed next to my son, I had such a wonderful surprise. At 11:00 p.m., in walked Steve, with a cup of coffee in his hand. He said, "The coffee is too cold to drink, but I thought you might like the company." For the first time in three years I had someone to sit with me while my son was in the hospital. For three years I had walked this journey with my son alone, with no one to hold me up when I was unsteady. No one to dry my tears when I was sad. No one to keep me company when I was lonely. No one to tell me it would be okay, when all signs say it wouldn't. I was grateful that I had found someone who loved me, not in spite of it all, but because of it all. I finally got my cup of coffee. A coffee from Starbucks, no less.

WE AREN'T LEAVING

The results of the EEG were significantly abnormal, and indicated that there may be a structural defect, which brought us to today's MRI. What I hate about the MRI is that he needed to be under anesthesia. What I like about the MRI is the answers it provides. Andrew was in super-good spirits when we left the house this morning. Like most kids, I think he enjoyed the day off from school.

We drove up to Children's Hospital Orange County for the MRI. They let me hold Andrew as they administered the anesthesia. That may have been good for him, but it was not good for me. His little body went so limp, it felt like he was dying in my arms. It was horrible! Then I obsessed the entire time he was in there that he had died.

I was a full-time job for Steve that day. I was a hot, weepy, mess. Once in recovery, Andrew had a hard time coming out of the anesthesia. The nurses seemed to be in a big hurry to get us out the door. Andrew's speech was so slurred that I couldn't understand him.

Finally it dawned on me that the nurses thought this was how he came in. I said to Steve, "I think they think Andrew came in this way. That's why they're trying so hard to get rid of us."

Steve called the nurse over and said to her, "We aren't going anywhere until he can talk to us. We are going to leave with the same kid we brought in."

After about 45 minutes, Andrew's speech became very clear, but he was having trouble balancing. At that point we all just wanted to go home. We let them bring Andrew to the car in a wheelchair. In the parking garage I thanked Steve for being the heavy. He acknowledged the importance of being the best advocate you can be for your children. He agreed that the staff at the hospital must have assumed, based on Andrew's medical chart, that his speech was impaired when he arrived, and that's why they were trying to speed us out of recovery. I'm happy to say, we left with the same kid we brought.

NATURE FINDS A WAY

My doctor thought I was too old to be having a baby. I wasn't even 40! I was reasonably offended by this remark. He sent me for all kinds of testing. I thought that this baby was going to be good for all of us. That being said, I now have a new kind of worry. I had my other kids so close. Sophia was already born, and I figured I was already done having kids by the time Andrew was diagnosed with autism. Mindful of that diagnosis, this was the first baby I'd have to worry about possibly also having autism.

While the doctor had his set of concerns, autism was my main concern. I knew that autism is four times more prevalent in boys than girls. I was having a girl. The troubling news was, siblings of autistic children have a 25 percent diagnosis rate. Good news; different gene pool for baby girl. The reality was, while I was concerned, I was just too busy to obsess about something that had not happened, regarding a baby that had not yet been born. I had three other kids to raise, and there was no extra time in the day to focus on this. Plus, the toothpaste was already out of the tube. It is what it is.

MOST QUALIFIED

Andrew wanted to play T-ball. Like everything else, if he could ask me to do it, I'll make it happen. I figured that this could help him learn to catch and throw a ball, a necessity for any little boy, and a skill he is lacking. I went to the parent meeting to meet the coach. You could have knocked me over with a feather. The coach was a woman, and her daughter is on the team. She talked about league rules, practice schedule, snack schedule, and her coaching philosophy for this age and skill level. At the end of the meeting she asked if anyone had any questions. This dad raised his hand and, brace yourself, actually asked, "What exactly makes you qualified to coach T-ball?" Without missing a beat she said, "I went to college on an athletic scholarship to play women's softball. I played and was a member of the United States Women's Olympic Softball Team. Four years later, I coached the United States Women's Olympic Softball Team. I'm pretty sure that makes me the most qualified one here to coach five and six year olds playing T-ball." Are you kidding me?? I love this woman!!

MEDICAL RELEASE

I knew if I called on the phone, my doctor would say no. So I drove over to his office to get a medical release so I could fly, pregnant, to Arizona. My mom called and asked me to come. My father was deathly ill, and I was 37 weeks pregnant. To my surprise, he was receptive to my request. My doctor just wanted to call and talk to my dad's doctor, and asked me to wait in his office. It didn't take him long at all. He told me that he had lost his father and didn't have the opportunity to say good-bye, and he didn't want to take that opportunity away from me.

We had an agreement that if I went into labor I would stay in Arizona and have the baby there. With my sitter in place to watch the kids, Steve and I headed to Arizona the next day. We went right from the airport to the hospital, and spent all of Thursday at the hospital. At the end of visiting hours my mom, my sister, Steve and I decided where to meet for dinner. While walking to the car in the hospital parking lot my hip popped out. I knew I was in trouble, but I kept it to myself. I just dropped into bed that night from physical and emotional exhaustion.

Friday morning I suggested to Steve that we change our return flight to sometime Saturday instead of Sunday night. He kept asking why. I just said that it was too emotional a time when I was supposed to be so happy about a new baby, to be so sad about losing my dad. He suggested we wait and see how I felt on Saturday. I sat in the hospital all day Friday, hoping to slow down the inevitable. By Saturday morning I knew I was in labor, but my water hadn't broken. I just kept hanging on to that one fact. I told Steve to please change our flight. I needed to go home.

We went to the hospital to spend my last day with my dad. As I said my goodbyes, I told my dad he had to hang on long enough to meet the baby. He promised to do his best. My contractions at this point were far enough apart that I knew I could make it back to San Diego. My mom, my sister, Steve and I went for a quick dinner on the way to the airport. During dinner I broke down in tears. It had been a long time since anyone had seen me so emotional. I begged them to get me on the next flight. I had to get home to San Diego. They were begging me to just check into the hospital and have the baby there.

I couldn't do it. I didn't want to be so far away from my kids, just in case something was wrong with the baby. I didn't want my kids in San Diego and me in Arizona. We got to the airport and my family was going to wait until the plane was in the air, in case I changed my mind. Steve was trying to talk me out of getting on the plane, using my germ phobia to scare me about having the baby mid-flight. My water hadn't broken.

As the plane began to taxi away from the gate, the flight attendant began her announcements. Steve missed the part about landing in San Diego before going on to San Jose. All he heard was San Jose. He jumped up and started to flip out. He thought we were on the wrong plane. Everyone sitting around us straightened him out. I didn't have to say a word. As a matter of fact, I asked nicely if he could just give me an hour of quiet to re-group. Mid-flight I needed to use the restroom. The snarky flight attendant asked how I could possibly get medical clearance to fly (mind you, I had only gained 18 pounds; how pregnant could I look?). I looked right at her and said, "My dad is dying. I wanted to say good-bye." I turned on my heels and went right back to my seat.

As we started to descend into San Diego, Steve asked if I wanted the flight attendants to have an ambulance waiting. No thanks. I thought all the fuss would elevate my blood pressure and...my water hadn't broken. We got off the plane, got our luggage and I waited curbside for Steve to pick me up. Only problem, there was a nighttime bicycle race that was coursing through the airport. I am not joking. As Steve tells it, he had to weave his way across the street, through a long-awaited gap in the bicyclists to get to the car, and that took time. Apparently getting out of the parking lot was worse. Steve rolled his window down yelling, "My wife's having a baby! My wife's having a baby!" honking his horn, edging his way into traffic to make the bikes make room for his car.

Once out of the airport, we had to stop for the train. I couldn't make this up. I had to laugh. Once on the freeway, he asked if we should head home. Uh, no, I need to go to the hospital. I'm in labor. He dropped me at the hospital, and with a list in his hand, headed home to get all the things I would need for the new baby.

At eleven o'clock he called me. "You sound so good," he said.

"Yes, I do," I replied. "I've had my epidural."

"What?"

"Yes, Steve, I'm having the baby. And if you want to be here, I suggest coming back to the hospital." Early the next morning, beautiful baby Bianca came into the world. There is nothing in this world like holding a brand-new baby. It's euphoric. I hope to enjoy every moment of life's most precious gift.

ROAD TRIP

My dad didn't die, and had actually been released from the hospital. He said he feels like the cat with nine lives. We are taking a road trip to Arizona so my dad can meet the new baby.

All the logistics, planning and packing that go into a trip like this with all the kids is worth it. The kids can hardly wait to show off their new baby sister. None of my kids were ever only children, so all they have ever known is being part of a big family. A new baby to them is just, the more the merrier. I know that my mom is happy that we're coming so she can get her hands on the new baby.

I can't wait for the moment my dad can hold baby Bianca. I know what holding a new baby does for me, and I'm hoping that my dad feels the same way. What a blessing this new baby is for our family. For Steve, this new baby girl is helping to fill a painful void created when one of his sisters passed away a few years ago, taken too soon. Babies have the powerful ability to heal, and I know that our baby Bianca is up for the job.

LOOKING GOOD

The face of autism had changed for me that school year. In the past I was preoccupied with the challenges. But this year, I was embracing the strengths. This year, my son played on a "typical" soccer team and T-ball team. He learned new physical skills, and had kind and loving people encouraging him and coaching him. While he continued to struggle socially, he was expanding his areas of interest. My dad taught him to read the statistics and box scores in the sports section, and Andrew's ability to understand and regurgitate is amazing. He will be popular in any sports bar.

Then, I agreed to allow Andrew to have a language-based IQ test. He is exceptionally bright. While much of his language was still very scripted, he has the ability to use it appropriately, and his vocabulary is phenomenal. I love that he will hug me and occasionally hold my hand. He loves his sisters, and doesn't have a mean bone in his body. Andrew is a people pleaser; he doesn't want to disappoint. No one worked harder in the classroom.

Still, he operated in Andrew Standard Time, instead of Pacific Standard Time. Andrew had expanded his dietary palate that year. That year had been a big year of change and growth. He demonstrated that small changes in his routine can be tolerated. I didn't say he was happy about it, but he was learning to be more flexible. The biggest success for that year…he wore tennis shoes to school and kept them on all day, every day. Equally amazing, he wore underwear, and used the bathroom successfully, not one accident. I'd say we had a lot to be happy about. Things were looking good as we were heading into first grade.

SLIDING INTO FIRST

One year ago today I stood on the elementary school blacktop to watch Isabella climb the stairs as a kindergartner, and slide down the slide into first grade. Today I stood on the same blacktop, unable to hold back my tears as I watched my favorite son (sure, my only son) climb the stairs with his special-ed kindergarten class and slide down into a mainstream first grade classroom. That's right, MAINSTREAM!!!! I was crying tears of pride for all the hard work, sacrifice, dedication, tenacity, and perseverance that made this day possible. My son has an unbreakable spirit. He did it. I was undoubtedly the proudest mom on the blacktop.

FIRST GRADE (AGE 6-7)
2009-2010

MISS M

It was the week before school was to start, and I took Andrew down to the school to meet his teacher and get familiar with his new classroom. For a kid like Andrew, change is hard, so I really appreciated that he could get this one-on-one time with his teacher. Let's be honest, the first day of school can be overwhelming for the best of us. So the back story on Miss M is that she was an accredited special education teacher, a credential not lost on me. In addition to having a qualified teacher, Andrew would have an aide in the classroom that would be shared with three other students. The plan was to keep him in the classroom for instructional time, and to pull him out for speech therapy and occupational therapy.

Miss M met us at the classroom door with a big smile for Andrew. He went right past her and began looking immediately for his desk. Thank goodness he was placed in the front of the class. For some reason I thought he'd do better there. He quickly looked through his desk and asked, "Exactly where do you keep the silent reading books? I'd like to see your classroom library." That's my son, right down to business. This was Miss M's cue. She walked him over to the bookshelves and immediately had a connection with him. They must've talked about books for over ten minutes. I had never seen Andrew engage in a two-way conversation with a virtual stranger like that before. I thought we were off to a great start. He reluctantly followed her for the rest of the classroom tour. She was so soft-spoken in comparison to his teachers in the past, I was wondering how he would do.

I knew from past experience that he really responded to high affect, or someone extremely animated. At the end of the meeting, he couldn't think of anything else that he wanted to know about his teacher or classroom. I hung back for the entire meeting. I kept my mouth shut, and was just a good listener. On the way out the door she spoke to me for the first time. "He's in good hands this year. I will love him like he's my own." That's all I needed to hear; that's all that mattered.

As Andrew and I walked to the car I put my arm around him and said, "I am proud of you, son. You did it! A mainstream classroom. This is really going to be a great year for you. I expect great things from you this year."

"I can do it, Mom," Andrew said. Choking back tears, I couldn't say another word. Words cannot describe how I felt. If someone had told me three years ago that my son would be placed in a mainstream classroom, I wouldn't have believed it. I wanted it, I hoped and prayed for it, I worked hard for it, but it's Andrew who achieved it. Miss M: M for mainstream.

S-WORD

It doesn't happen very often, but tonight it was just Andrew and myself in the car. We were driving home, listening to the radio. A public service announcement came on about the importance of talking to your kids about the "S-word." About 10 minutes later the commercial came on again. Somewhere from the back row of the car I heard Andrew say, "Mom, I know what the S-word is."

"Oh, really? What is it?" I asked.

"It's sex, Mom," he announced.

"WHAT?" I exclaimed.

"Yeah, it's sex. I know all about it," he said coolly.

"Ummm, what exactly do you know about the S-word?" I asked.

"EVERYTHING. I am six, you know." I erupted into laughter. Six? Sex? Glad six is the S-word he knows all about.

WHAT WAITING ROOMS HAVE TAUGHT ME

What waiting rooms have taught me:

Any professional worth seeing is worth waiting for.

No matter how bad you think you have it, someone has it worse.

I'm not going to focus on what he can't do, I'm going to focus on all the things he can do.

For every sacrifice I've made, some other parent has made ten more.

Every special child comes from a special family.

Be open to suggestions, but you know your child best.

Trust your instinct.

The kid melting down today may be your kid tomorrow.

Ask for the help you need.

Know your limitations.

Do your homework and put in the hard work.

Be your child's best advocate; your child is counting on you.

Autism is an equal opportunity offender; it crosses all races and socio-economic classes.

What waiting rooms have taught my kids:

I don't negotiate with terrorists. If you want to talk about it, great. If you want to cry…forget it.

Don't underestimate how far cute and well-mannered can get you.

Keep your hands to yourself.

Play nicely.

Clean up after yourself.

The rules do apply to you.

Don't stare.

Say please and thank you.

Answer adults when they talk to you.

The kid screaming and ripping the toy out of your hands can't help it. Use the opportunity to demonstrate how generous you are.

When someone is crying, see if you can help. Use the opportunity to show how empathetic you are.

Don't ignore the kid talking to you because you can't understand what they are saying. Use the opportunity to demonstrate your ability to problem solve.

ALWAYS BE PREPARED

All last year Andrew couldn't understand why he couldn't join Isabella's Daisy Troop. I wasn't sure if he couldn't understand, or didn't want to understand. I kept assuring him that as soon as he was old enough, he could join the Boy Scouts. What I really couldn't understand was why Isabella's troop leader wouldn't let him do a craft every once in a while, or have a snack with the girls. Oh well, the time had come...I signed Andrew up for Cub Scouts. I took him to get his uniform and handbook. I can't get him out of the uniform, and he carries the handbook with him wherever he goes. He has already read the handbook from beginning to end.

I know what he is really looking forward to is the prospect of camping. Unfortunately for my kids, my idea of camping is a hotel without room service. No, seriously, this mom will not be camping. I thought that this was going to be so good for Andrew. First, he had been looking forward to this for an entire school year. Second, he was going to be doing what boys and men do. What that is, I cannot tell you. What I can tell you is that my dad was an Eagle Scout, and I know some of his fondest childhood memories are from being a scout. I only hope that I'm not the only mom there. Maybe I'll learn some survival skills. What's the motto: "Be Prepared." Look, Boy Scouts of America, you've got nothing on me. Mother of four, I know a few things about always being prepared. Prepared for what, I don't know; but I'm prepared.

LUNCH TABLES

I did a pop-in this week during lunch. The school the kids go to has this crazy nutritional policy that they follow. Not allowable snacks are soda, candy, gum, fried chips (potato, Doritos, Cheetos, etc.), no food at birthday or personal celebrations, and no daily food rewards. Seriously? What kind of institution takes the treats out of birthdays? If we don't have some junk food to look forward to, what is there in life? Ugh! What kid honestly wants to celebrate their birthday with a celery stick, or a fruit kabob? Just another slice of California crazy.

I showed up at the lunch tables with a bag of Fritos, as risqué as I was willing to get. After all, I did have to live in this neighborhood. I brought the bag for Andrew to share with his friends. I just wanted to see how it was all going for him, and meet the classmates that he had lunch with. His new friends. Well, it appeared as if the phrase, "birds of a feather, flock together," holds true. Amazingly enough, Andrew appeared to have naturally migrated to the two other kids in his class with special needs. I will say this; both Andrew and I were extremely popular with our bag of Fritos to share.

As the bell rang, Miss M came over to check in and I shared my observation with her. She confirmed. I hoped that recess improved for Andrew. I knew he was having trouble on the playground. Isabella told me that he waited patiently for a turn at four square and that the other kids keep changing the rules so that they never get out, and therefore he never gets a turn to play. I couldn't believe that the playground supervisors let this go on, but I knew it was true. I didn't worry about Andrew in the classroom. He does really well in a highly structured environment. I worried about him during unstructured, unsupervised segments of the day. Wish they could have treats at school. It could even the playing field for a kid like Andrew.

FORGIVENESS

Along with a mainstream classroom comes mainstream activities. Andrew desperately wanted to play soccer, so I did what any mom would do. I signed him up for soccer. Like any good bully, the coach's son sensed right off the bat that Andrew was the weak link. During practice the coach paired up boys to scrimmage against each other. As Andrew was paired up and ready to play, the coach's son yelled out to the other kid, "You got this one, you're scrimmaging the team retard!" It was like an out-of-body experience. I was lucky I didn't end up on the five o'clock news. I started to run across the field, yelling, "He's not retarded, he's autistic! He's not retarded, he's autistic!"

My worst fear was playing itself out. This kid said out loud what I knew people were thinking. The rest of the practice I stood on the sideline and cried, tears just streaming down my face. As we walked to the car after practice, I heard a small voice behind me. "Andrew's mom? Andrew's mom?" I stopped. Sure enough, it was the coach's son. He said, "I'm really sorry about what I said about your son today."

With all eyes on me I said, "I forgive you."

When we got to the car, and after I had the baby in her car seat, Isabella came over to me and wrapped her arms around me. While she was giving me a hug she said, "Mom, I'm proud of you." Sometimes the opportunity presents itself to walk the walk.

COUGH-COUGH

I had picked up Andrew early from school three days this week for his constant coughing. The nurse informed me today that he can't come back without a doctor's note, confirming that he is not ill. Ill? Seriously? No fever, no runny nose, no sore throat, the throat isn't red, no earache and no visible signs of illness. A dry cough, that's it, and for that I need a doctor's note? The pediatrician asked him to count to 50. He did it, without coughing once. Diagnosis: a tic. He wrote the note that the school demanded and asked me to wait while he called Dr. Donnelly. Five minutes later we were on the road and on our way to see Dr. Donnelly.

At the time, I thought maybe the coughing was a side effect from the epilepsy medicine. Wrong, so wrong. This is why there are no initials after my name, like the all-important M.D. you need to practice medicine. Keep in mind, they do refer to it as the "practice" of medicine. At the conclusion of today's visit with Dr. Donnelly, we had yet another something to add to our growing list of concerns. Autism, epilepsy and now...Tourettes. This was a hard pill for me to swallow. I understood that this is about the age of onset. I could actually be objective and say that the motor tics were obvious to me, like the facial grimace and his hand shooting up in the air. I didn't realize until today that the phonic tics are involuntary, that the sounds are produced by moving air through the nose, mouth or throat—THE COUGHING! I felt so bad for asking him to stop coughing. He couldn't control it. The girls bugged him like crazy about it. I guessed we were all going to have to learn to ignore it. The coughing was here to stay.

LIVING THE DREAM

I wanted Andrew to be a doctor. He wanted to be a professional football player. Indeed, the next Tom Brady. My son, the one who has so many neurological challenges, wanted to play football. I had never wanted the job of killing someone's dream or crushing their spirit. I did not apply for that job. But it appeared that I got it without even interviewing. This desire to play football was unrealistic. I never said no, I just continued to put it off. However, I thought I had found a compromise—Flag Football. This was a genius solution. I'm not sure who gets credit for being the genius, Andrew or myself, since he actually brought the flyer home from school. He starts this Sunday, and he is super enthusiastic. This is perfect for me—no weekly practice, just thirty minutes before each one-hour game. The girls can play at the park for an hour and a half while Andrew lives out his football fantasy. I love it when I can figure out something that makes everyone happy. It's not quite football, but it's close enough for Andrew. He's living the dream. One that I have managed not to kill.

HONESTY

Honesty. It's an interesting thing, because Andrew can't lie. If I wanted to get to the bottom of any situation in my house, I asked Andrew. Recently, we had an episode which was the perfect platform for me to deliver the "importance of honesty" speech. Before I began the speech, I felt that I should disclose something to my kids that I hadn't been honest about. "I'm not really twenty-one," I announced. Everyone looked shocked by my announcement. Even as I gave my speech on honesty to my kids, it felt hypocritical. I mean, Andrew was honest, but sometimes the truth hurts. I didn't like to hear that my breath smells or that my nail polish color is hideous. Like many autistic children, he pointed out the defects. Andrew blurted out the obvious: things that are the truth, but sometimes (more often than not) should go unsaid. My mom likes to refer to it as not having the ability to filter or screen. I only hope that he can acquire this skill. He can appear rude or ill mannered, abrasive even.

While Andrew doesn't lie, he also assumes that other people are as honest as he is. This leads to another host of problems. He is overly trustful, and can easily be taken advantage of. He is easy to manipulate. I worried about how easy it would be for him to find himself in unimaginable situations at the hands of the wrong people. I watched him like a hawk, and I think it would be crazy not to. Andrew was receiving an award at school for Honesty. I didn't know anyone who deserved that award more. While I celebrated the success of his having strong character, I worried about his inability to see the dark side of people. I worry more than I can celebrate. Honestly.

PLAY BALL

I have officially fulfilled my fantasy of having a child play professional sports. Andrew was part of Little League Day at Petco Park. He paraded around the field with his baseball team, stayed on the field for the National Anthem and then joined us in our seats for today's Padres game. I was nervous about today for a lot of different reasons. I wasn't sure if he could handle the crowds of people, the noise level, the smell of the food, all the organized chaos. To my amazement, he did it, and he loved it. I used a lot of baseball analogies when I talked about life with Andrew, maybe because of his love for the game, or maybe because of what the game represented to me. Either way, just like a batter waiting to swing at a pitch, my hope for Andrew is that he connects.

ARE YOU MY SISTER?

We had an unfortunate episode with our neighbors today. The kids were over playing at our house, and the little girl from next door came into the kitchen looking very upset. "Andrew keeps asking me if I'm his sister, and I don't think he is funny." So as I was trying to explain to her that sometimes Andrew doesn't recognize familiar faces, I could see her frustration. "But he keeps asking me over and over and I keep telling him no." I just decided to cut my losses and take her home. I love my neighbors. Her mom was super understanding and felt bad. I just didn't want to overstep my bounds, and thought it would be better to let her explain Andrew's inquiries in whatever way she wanted to handle it with her kids.

The reality is, it's the seizures that cause the confusion for Andrew, not the autism. I knew how I explained it to the girls, but I just didn't think it was my place to explain it to someone else's kids, especially little kids. I didn't want to scare them. I didn't want them to treat him differently. It was so hard for me, I never really know. Do you tell people up front? Do you wait for something to happen and then explain why? What do you tell kids? What can kids understand? What can adults understand? What do they really want to understand? Lots of questions, lots of opinions, and who knows the answers?

STANDING ON SECOND

First grade flew by. Andrew did an amazing job this school year. Andrew will be placed in a mainstream second-grade classroom WITHOUT an aide for fall. This time, a male teacher. While he struggled socially this year, he did a tremendous job academically. His teacher was so patient and kind and really knew how to bring out the best in him, while holding him to a high standard. The aide that was assigned to him did not have to intervene on his behalf even once the entire school year. Not one time. He did it, he really did it. Andrew required a tremendous amount of over management, but he really exceeded my expectations for the school year.

I was planning to have a tutor come all summer so that he wouldn't slip behind, as he has a tendency to do while on any break from his routine. He had two friends this year at school that he really seemed to play nicely with. He was invited to a birthday party. He went on a playdate. He ordered lunch from the cafeteria all school year long and ate whatever was served to him. Besides not wanting to wear a jacket when it was cold out, we didn't have any clothes or shoe issues this year. He didn't have any seizures or episodes of confusion at school this year. He participated in all classroom activities, including performing in front of parents and schoolmates.

While he had a lot of successes, we had a few setbacks. The epilepsy and the inability to control the seizures was worrisome. The onset of Tourette was an unwelcome surprise. I was looking forward to a break from school and a break from all the therapy. This was the first summer Andrew and the girls would be going to Arizona without me. This was our first real break from each other. Ten days. Ten days for me of nowhere to be, nothing to do. I was nervous about the time away from Andrew. It would probably be good for the both of us. We accomplished a lot this school year, and I was looking forward to fall with anticipation. Standing safely on second, third doesn't look that hard to reach.

SECOND GRADE (AGE 7-8)
2010-2011

PARTY AT THE PARK

This was the first year that I felt up to hosting a birthday party for Andrew with friends. In the past, we've done a family only party that involved a great outing, like Disneyland, so he wouldn't be asking why he doesn't get a party. Interestingly enough, he had never asked for a party. Hmmm. Anyway, I decided to have the party at the park close to our home. He wanted a bounce house, so I rented one for the day. I rented tables, chairs, ordered pizza and invited his entire class and the kids next door. Besides my kids and the kids next door, there were only three kids from his class that came.

Lucky for Andrew, he seemed oblivious to it all. For me, it made my heart hurt. Isn't that what parents worry about, throwing a party for their kids and no one wanting to come? Well, I had countless sleepless nights over that one, only to have it almost come true. The good thing was that between my kids and the kids next door, that's a party of seven. True to form, Andrew didn't notice at all. He spent most of the party jumping in the bounce house. I could hardly get him to join us to eat pizza. He had been looking forward to his batman cake and, of course, the presents. It had all the elements of a special day for him, not to underestimate the importance of having his two friends there. In my mind the measure of a successful birthday party was based on the number of people that showed up, and Andrew couldn't have cared less. For Andrew, he had his first party with good friends, good food, a great cake and he got presents. He couldn't have been happier. I have to accept that the standard by which I measure things is just not important to Andrew. If it isn't important to Andrew, then it shouldn't be important to me. The birthday party at the park was a success for everyone, even if it wasn't the blowout I had imagined. It was just what Andrew wanted, and that's really all that mattered.

AFTER-SCHOOL MOVIE

The PTA had organized an after-school movie, and all the kids wanted to go. I was very nervous about this. What if Andrew wandered off? What if he couldn't handle all the kids in the cafeteria, the noise, the smells? I had to pull the girls aside and give them the "I expect you to look out for Andrew" speech. Then I worried that the girls' friends would make fun of or tease Andrew. What about all the unsupervised, unstructured time? Could he do it? Well, I decided to give it a try. What was the worst thing that could happen? I shouldn't even say that out loud. Amazingly enough, they all did it, and had a great time. Andrew sat with Sophia. They got their snack and sat near one of the sides that seemed quieter, Sophia reported. Not one problem. Who knew? Not me. I think that it helped that it was a movie that all the kids liked. Who doesn't enjoy a slice of pizza, juice box and some popcorn?

The movie was good, the snacks were good, and two of the three kids sat together. Sounds to me like a pretty good time. This was a huge success for Andrew. I knew he was amazed that I even let him go in the first place, and I'm sure he tried his hardest so that he could have more independence in the future. Baby steps. One step forward, that's all that matters.

BUMP IN THE NIGHT

The sound was so loud that as I leapt from my bed, I could only imagine the worst. It sounded like a car had crashed through the garage door. I ran downstairs to see what had happened. I was about halfway down the stairs when I heard moaning coming from Andrew's room. I found him on the floor. He'd had a seizure that was so violent, it had thrown him from his bed and into his closet doors, causing the doors to fall off their tracks. My heart broke for him. I wished that I could trade his brain with mine. He was disoriented, confused, listless.

I called Dr. Donnelly and left a message with the on-call service. I just climbed in bed with him and laid there, rubbing Andrew's back, patiently waiting for the doctor to call. I didn't want to call 9-1-1. I didn't want an ambulance here in the middle of the night. I just hated that the medication wasn't working. I just wanted it all to go away. All of it. I knew what an episode like this meant. More medication, more testing, another hospital stay. The logistics could be overwhelming on a good day. But in the darkness of night, my mind always goes to dark places; really dark places. What kind of life could Andrew have with seizures like this? How would he ever live independently? How could I ever stop worrying about him? Who would ever love him like I do? In moments like this, I'd say to myself, it could be so much worse; but really, what would that look like? This looked pretty bad to me, especially in the dark of night.

THE BIG APPLE

We were all headed to New York for Steve's niece's bat mitzvah. The logistics of this trip alone were enough to give me a nervous breakdown, not to mention all the concerns about how Andrew would do with the change in scenery. I'd been talking about the trip for a month now in great detail. I'd described the hotel, what the service will be like, what the party will be like, whose familiar faces the kids will see. We arranged a baby sitter for the parts of the weekend we didn't think Bianca or Andrew could handle. I was prepared to leave any portion of the festivities to take Andrew back to the hotel. The night of the big party came, and Andrew was dressed and ready to go. We got to the venue. It was multi-level, with all the pre-party games on one level. I could see Andrew starting to panic. The girls ran off immediately to participate.

Andrew held back. Eventually he joined in, but you could see he was overwhelmed. When they ushered us downstairs for dinner and dancing, Andrew really had a hard time transitioning. He wanted to sit in the very back far corner of the room, closest to the kitchen. He didn't want to join the kids for dinner. I sat with Andrew in that corner for over an hour. I couldn't tell you how many people came by to ask if we were okay. I just wanted to wait and see if he could acclimate, or if we needed to call it a night. Slowly but surely, he did it. He eventually wanted to get something to eat and, before long, I even saw him playing with some of the other kids. I thought the noise level was hard for him, and with all the flashing lights, I was surprised he didn't have a seizure with all of the sensory overload. But he didn't. He actually made it through the entire evening. As hard as it was for him, it was just as hard for me. I knew that this would be a hard evening for him, and I tried my best to prepare him for all the unexpected. In the taxi on the way back to the hotel Andrew spontaneously said, "Mom, you were right, I did have a good time." Wow, mission accomplished for Operation Big Apple.

WEDDING DAY

Steve and I had been planning our wedding for a long time now. Every chance we had, we'd take the kids with us, to help make them feel like they were part of the planning. Sophia came to me the other evening very upset about my pending name change. She wanted to know if, when I change my name, that means that I'm not her mom anymore; if it means we won't be family since we don't have the same name. I felt so bad. You never know what kids are thinking about. I explained that I will always be her mom, no matter what my last name is. Just like someday when she gets married, she might want to take her husband's last name, and that won't mean that she isn't my daughter anymore. I planned to have the girls be my flower girls and have my dad and Andrew give me away. I felt so blessed to be able to have my dad attend. He's like the cat with nine lives. I felt like he was living on borrowed time. I thought my dad and my son giving me away would be symbolic in a sense. Andrew was excited about getting to wear a tux. He looked so handsome. He acknowledged that he was nervous about walking me down the aisle and having every-one looking at him. I assured him that if he just focused on the end of the aisle, he wouldn't notice anyone looking at him. As we stood at the back of the ballroom, he wanted to hold my hand. At the end of the aisle, before he went to sit down, he squeezed my hand three times, our code for "I Love You." He did it, he managed to walk me down the aisle. What a great accomplishment.

At the reception, he sat at the kids table all evening and even danced. Steve's nieces and nephews surrounded him; sat with him and all the kids. They seemed to have a wonderful time. I gave a speech to my sister. Steve's son gave the best man speech. To my surprise, Steve serenaded me and gave a moving speech.

At the end of the evening, when it was time for him to go home, Andrew started to cry. "Mom, I just don't want this night to be over."

As I hugged him tightly, I whispered in his ear, "Me neither, Andrew." You know, you never know where life is going to take you, but I am proud of my kids and their ability to adapt. I think that they may be more flexible than I am. The kids and I are truly blessed to have a man in our lives that loves us all just the way we are. It was truly a magical day, not just for myself, but my kids, too. I couldn't ask for more than that.

THE BIG MOVE

After months of discussion, planning, packing, painting, and remodeling, moving day was here. We were moving to a new neighborhood, to a new life, in a sense. The kids and I had moved a lot, and I was hoping that this would be our last move. I had learned the hard way to never make promises, so I wouldn't say for sure, but in my mind, this was our last move. We weren't officially going to change schools until the fall, so I would be driving the kids back and forth for the remainder of the school year. This seemed to have made the concept of moving easier on everyone. I will say for all the moves, the kids had never had to change schools. Do I get extra credit points for that? I do on the report card I'm keeping for myself. I had been trying to sell this move hard to the girls because I knew that they could help me sell it to Andrew.

Packing was very hard for him. He is a hoarder, and every last scrap of paper holds special meaning for him. I tried to throw out stuff when the kids weren't around, but it had not been easy for them to part with their things. With every move, I tried to lighten the load, so to speak. I was actually starting to wonder if the moving was really the hardest on me. Kids are amazingly adaptable, much more than adults. We were moving into a beautiful home, much bigger than anything we had ever lived in before. The neighborhood was amazing, and the school was phenomenal. If Isabella hadn't been so adamant about finishing out the school year, I would have tried to move them before school was out for the summer. I knew that some people would say that it's easier on kids if they can at least get familiar with the school and kids before they break for summer. I'm not sure about any of it, but we were finishing the school year where we were.

I thought that this transition was actually going to work out best for everyone, including me. We could get comfortable with the new house and new neighborhood while having the benefit of going back to our familiar surroundings for the next few months. Before the school year ended, I was planning to take the kids over to their new school to meet the principal and take a tour. This move was like a fresh start for us. No one knew us or all of our business. I told the kids it's the opportunity for all of us to make new friends and create a new life. It was definitely a big move. The move came with apprehension, some dislocation, but overall, a lot of excitement and enthusiasm. Like I tell the kids with every move, it's a different four walls, but it's the same us. We always have each other.

PLAY DATES ARE OVERRATED

So, against my better judgment, Andrew talked me into a play date at his friend's house. I preferred to have kids over at my house, that way I could supervise and jump in when assistance was needed. You know, because I love Andrew just the way he is, sometimes I forget that he just isn't like other kids. I spoke to the mother on the phone and gave her full disclosure on all the issues we have going on. She assured me that she was up for the task, and was looking forward to having Andrew over. I gave the speech 642 times to Andrew about hands to ourselves, use appropriate language, please use good manners, and last but not least, use good judgment.

I'm not sure what seven-year-old has good judgment, but I thought I would throw it in there for good measure. Andrew went home with the friend after school and was planning to stay until five thirty. Things must've gone smoothly, because I didn't hear from the mother prior to driving over to pick him up. Upon arrival she assured me that everyone had played nicely. They had an after-school snack and had gone to the park for a while before returning home to play. As we were standing in her foyer talking, a blood curdling scream came from the upstairs. I didn't recognize the sound as one of Andrew's. Her younger son came down the stairs in tears with a humongous welt in the middle of his forehead. I began searching for Andrew. I just knew he was to blame. I found him hiding under his friend's bed. I grabbed him by the ankle and pulled him out.

"What exactly happened?" I asked.

"My friend told me to hit his brother with the drum stick," he answered.

"What? Why would you do that?" I asked.

"Because my friend told me to," he answered my rhetorical question.

"Oh, Andrew. You must know better than that. Please go find his little brother and apologize," I instructed.

Andrew found the little boy crying on his mom's lap. He apologized just like I had asked him to. Then I said to him, "What do you say to your friend's mom?"

"I'm sorry your son asked me to hurt your other son," he said. God help me. Am I in an episode of the *Twilight Zone*? Did my son really just say that to this woman? I could have died of embarrassment.

The mom looked right at Andrew and said, "Good point, Andrew." I could not have apologized any more than I did, kicking myself the whole time for getting sucked into this idea of a play date. Then the mom gave full disclosure on the problems she was having in her own house. She had agreed to the play date because she herself was just glad that someone wanted to play with her son. We both agreed that maybe next time we'd just meet at the park, where they can't escape the eagle eyes of supervision. Birds of a feather, flock together. Sons and mothers.

GAME ON

Today was the big day, the Mother/Son Kickball Tournament. Andrew had been talking about this for weeks. I couldn't play last year because I was too pregnant, ready to pop any second. I had no excuse this year. As we were driving down to the school, Andrew was explaining the rules of the game to me. We had our matching baseball shirts on and were ready to play. First, we had our pictures taken, and then we checked in to find which field we would be playing on. I thought all Andrew really cared about was when he was going to get his treat, before or after the game. I settled for after, thinking if he had something to look forward to, I had a shot at him participating for the whole game.

As we were walking over to our assigned field Andrew said to me, "Mom, don't embarrass me today."

Wa-wa-what? "Game on son; game on." It was Moms vs. Boys. We tied the game, the good old-fashioned way. The boys and the moms played their hearts out. The moms didn't throw our game. We came on strong at the end so as not to get smeared. Not to brag, but I did kick a home run. As I rounded second base where Andrew was, I scooped him up and carried him to third. He loved it. I did him proud. He participated start to finish. He was engaged the entire time. I can honestly say, I had no interest in playing in this kickball tournament, but sometimes you have to take one for the team. The Mother/Son team, that is.

HEADING FOR THIRD

Second grade was an exhausting year for me. While Andrew success-fully completed the second grade without an aide, he was a full-time management nightmare for me. I eventually had a tutor coming twice a week to help with homework because it just seemed to drag on and on with me. Since Andrew operates in Andrew Standard Time, as opposed to Pacific Standard Time, it was necessary to modify the amount of at-home schoolwork that he needed to complete. The first week of school it was taking up to three hours to finish homework. No one needs to be doing homework for that amount of time. He did well on all the stan-dardize tests, but homework seemed to be a challenge.

He made two friends that year, both of whom are moving this summer, so they were all sad to say goodbye to each other. I came to accept this year that Andrew needed to be closely supervised in order to make sure that the play doesn't get too physically aggressive. It was interesting to me, because Andrew didn't have an aggressive personality at home or at school, just apparently on play dates. Andrew is attracted to the bullies on the playground. He really had a hard time this year with unsupervised, unstructured time at school.

By the end of the year I was dropping the kids off at the last minute and picking them up as the bell was ringing to dismiss them. He had a hard time medically. The seizures, nervous tics, and severe confusion made for a difficult academic year. Andrew had a history of one step forward, two steps back, and this year was no exception. This year I had to say, I felt defeated. I was looking forward to changing schools for fall. The new school seemed like a better fit for him in a lot of ways. The classrooms had a smaller number of kids. According to the principal, there were sev-eral other kids somewhere on the "spectrum." They had a ton of special-ized programs for social skills, cooking, speech therapy, and occupational therapy. They even had a garden for the kids to go into during recess.

Each year presented new challenges for Andrew, and I was just glad that we had the summer off to regroup and recharge. I thought both of us really needed it. This would be the first summer that I had not signed

Andrew up for any therapy. We were just going to take some time off. I could always play catch-up in the fall. I was looking forward to a fresh group of professionals working with Andrew. It would be good for him and for me. While we were heading for third, I was happy to be leaving second behind us.

THIRD GRADE (AGE 8-9)
2011-2012

ROBOT CAMP

I was doing something naughty. I signed Andrew up for Robot Camp and I did not say a word about the autism. I had to fill out the medical release form and, of course, I noted the epilepsy on the form, but I was trying a new strategy. I was not going to say a word unless something was brought up to me. He was so excited about this camp. The girls were going to tennis camp, and he did not want to play. Who can blame him? He was skin and bones. I wondered how long he could even hold up a tennis racket? Needless to say, the brain is the only muscle he wanted to exercise this summer. He picked the camp, and I agreed that it was a good choice for him.

Each child was going to engineer and build a robot. The company that runs the camp employs college-age engineering students. At pick-up today, the camp leader let me know that he was very impressed with Andrew. He told me that Andrew thinks like an engineer, he has an engineering mind. I'm so happy that someone is helping to fuel the creativity in Andrew. I could see Andrew beaming with pride for having his abilities praised. This would be a very positive experience for him.

When I decided to take the summer off from therapy, I also made the commitment to let Andrew help decide what new things he wanted to try. I was really impressed with Andrew's broadening range of interests. We would see how my experiment goes. I was trying to give us all a fresh start and give information to people on a need-to-know basis. In the past I had felt so isolated, that I just wanted to see how the new strategy worked. For better or worse, I was committed to giving it a try. In the meantime, maybe Andrew can engineer a way to keep the house clean and put the laundry away.

ARE YOU MY MOM?

Despite the swim lesson incident years ago, we had been spending our afternoons this summer swimming at the Pacific Athletic Club. I put Bianca in the childcare and the three big kids and I would go out to the pool for the afternoon. Today was no exception. I was standing on the side of the pool watching the girls dive for the swimming toys when Andrew came up next to me. I could tell he was confused. I asked him if he was okay. "Are you my mom?" he asked.

"Yes, I am," I replied. He said that he thought so, that I looked familiar to him. I led him back to the chairs and insisted that he lay down. I put some swim towels over him to help him warm up in the afternoon sun. I just sat next to him and rubbed his back. He has had bouts of confusion in the past, but he has never not known if I was his mom. My heart hurt; physically hurt. Thank goodness he did not have a seizure while he was in the swimming pool. It was reality checks like this that remind me how diligent I need to be around water.

What if he'd had a seizure and had drowned? What if I hadn't been standing at the side of the pool? Would the lifeguard have noticed with all the activity? Would one of the girls have noticed? I was just grateful that something inside Andrew prompted him to get out of the water. I worry about his safety, not just around water; but what if he had gone up to a stranger confused about who his mom was? What if he went somewhere with a stranger?

As I sat there rubbing his back in the warmth of the afternoon sun, I wished I could just rub all the confusion away. I just had to keep reminding myself to be grateful for all the things that went right today, instead of focusing on all the things that could go wrong. It was the constant battle in my brain. The fight between what went right and what could go wrong. I was grateful that Andrew instinctively knew I was his mom. Disaster averted.

GOALS

Andrew and I sat down to discuss his goals for this school year.

"Mom, this year I would like to have a meaningful friendship," he said.

"Me too, Andrew," I replied.

"No, seriously, Mom," he said.

"No, seriously, Andrew. It's hard to find a friend that really understands us the way we are. Not every friendship we have is going to be meaningful. I want the same thing, too. Not just for you, but for myself, too," I said.

"Oh, well, good luck, Mom. You're going to need it."

Good thing he's so cute.

MEET THE TEACHER

The big day had arrived. I took the kids to their new school to meet their teachers. We went from youngest to oldest today. Some days we go from oldest to youngest, with Andrew always in the middle. Sophia breezed in and out of her classroom, much more interested in playing on the playground. From the time we got out of the car, Andrew wanted to hold my hand. I could tell that he was nervous. He held my hand all the way through the door of his classroom. His teacher couldn't have been any nicer. She ran a tight ship, and held all the kids in her classroom to high standards. She was going to be perfect for Andrew. I really thought he'd flourish in this environment. She asked Andrew what he was looking forward to most this year. His answer, "I'd like to make a meaningful friendship." Me too, Andrew.

As we walked to Isabella's classroom, he decided that he wanted to go look in the school garden and would meet me in Isabella's classroom. Before he ran off I said to him, "I mean it, Andrew, that's my goal for this school year too. I would like to have a meaningful friendship." I sometimes think that Andrew and I are more alike than not. I'm not saying that I'm autistic, because I'm not. But I think if you boil human nature down to its simplest form, most of us want the same things. I don't think that some (not all) of Andrew's challenges are really that different than anybody else's. We want to know that we belong. We want to feel that people like us for who we are. We want to have meaningful relationships. I am hopeful that this is a successful year for everyone.

STUDY BUDDY

This new school had a great program called Study Buddies. They'd meet Mondays after school with a high school student that they have been paired up with. First they have a snack, then they do homework, then they play games on the playground together. Andrew had been paired up with the nicest, most outgoing high school boy. I couldn't be happier. One day a week I didn't have to do homework, and he was getting that one-on-one time from a male in a supervised setting: not to mention that his study buddy let me know he liked to babysit and is CPR certified. Are you kidding me? Does it get any better than this?

So we were going to have the study buddy over one evening a week. He was going to come early and eat dinner with us, and then stay to do an hour's worth of homework with Andrew. The principal at our new school was not a fan of homework, but wouldn't you know Andrew got the one teacher who is a firm believer in it. My one kid who takes forever to get the work done, is the only kid that has schoolwork to do. I hope you were counting. That's two days a week I'm not doing home-work. This move was the best thing that happened for the kids.

I asked Andrew how he was liking his new school. He started to cry. He told me that until this school, he didn't realize how mean the other kids were to him. So, he can tell the difference between positive and negative attention. I always wondered. My heart hurt for him. I told him that there were lots of nice kids just like him at the new school, and I just knew that he was going to be happy here. He nodded in agreement. "Plus," he said, "I have a big kid friend, my study buddy, who can't wait to come over to our house." I could see a confidence in Andrew that I had never seen before. I thought he really was fitting in, in a way he never had before.

WHY?

"Mom, why did God make me like this?" Andrew asked.

"Because God expects great things from you. You see the world differently so that you can be part of the solution, not the problem. God expects you to use all of your special gifts to make a difference in this world. Guess what? I expect that, too. I love you just the way you are, and I wouldn't change a thing about you. Well, maybe one thing. It would be nice if you could keep your Legos off the floor," I replied.

"Uggh, MOM!!" he exclaimed, exasperated with me.

"Well, they hurt to step on," I announced.

OPRAH LOVED ME THROUGH IT

I was listening to a group of moms at soccer today, talking about getting through hard times. One of the moms used an expression I had never heard before, but as of today I am making it my own. Referring to her early twenties she said, "My parents loved me through it." I love this. I started to think of all the challenges I've faced and who could I point to and use that expression.

After considerable thought I had to say…Oprah has loved me through some of my darkest hours. I used to record her show and watch it after I had gotten all the kids to bed at night. No matter what kind of day I'd had, I always found something to take away from every show I watched. Some days I laughed, some days I cried. But most days, I was grateful for my life just the way it was. No matter what challenges I was facing, someone was facing harder ones. No matter what kind of heartache I was experiencing, someone's heart hurt more. Some of life's hardest lessons, I got to learn the easy way…by watching them on television.

For the decade that Oprah was loving me through it, I became a better person. I accepted my reality, I did the hard work. I invested the time. I sacrificed the resources. I became grateful for all the things my life was. Even in my darkest hour, I truly found my attitude for gratitude. Every heartache, every obstacle, every challenge, I have learned to see as an opportunity for growth. What I really learned was to take good care of myself. Oprah certainly helped me with the knowledge and insight, but in reality…I too loved myself through it.

FLAWED STRATEGY

My new strategy regarding not telling people that Andrew is autistic had some significant flaws. I let him go on a playdate with a classmate that lived around the corner from us. The playdate wasn't scheduled to be that long, due to their after-school activities. Perfect. They walked him home, and while I was inside the house talking to the mother about our most recent kitchen remodel, disaster struck. The little boy came running in saying Andrew had broken his tooth. They had been throwing rocks at each other in the front yard, and one of the rocks had hit this little boy in the mouth and broken one of his teeth. One of his permanent front teeth. Ugh!!!! These two could not have been left unsupervised for more than five minutes; that's all it took. I couldn't stop apologizing. The mother assured me it was no big deal, they would just file the tooth down. Wow, Andrew broke one of her kid's front teeth and it's no big deal? After they left, I sent Andrew to his room. I wanted to calm down before I tried to talk to him. I sent the mother a long email, not just apologizing, but letting her know about the autism and epilepsy, which upon reflection I should have done upfront. If I wasn't embarrassed or ashamed, then why not just tell people in advance of a playdate? I guess I just didn't want it to define him. I didn't want people to look at him differently. In an effort to help Andrew have a "normal" childhood (whatever that is), I didn't want to have to lead with all the things that make him different.

This experience reminded me that full disclosure is essential if I want to set Andrew up to succeed. Other parents can't supervise properly or help facilitate if they aren't aware of the challenges. Andrew and I decided to bake brownies and bring them over to his friend to apologize for the tooth incident. Thankfully both child and mother were receptive to Andrew's apology. They assured Andrew that all was forgiven, and that they had moved on. My ex-husband actually had the best advice on the entire incident. He pointed out to me that boys play with rocks, they throw things at each other, they play war, wrestle and sometimes, some-one gets hurt. Accidents happen, autism or not. He actually said to me to quit beating myself up. This incident could have happened to anyone, and that it's more important for Andrew to have the opportunity to play like a boy with boys. You know what they say...boys will be boys. I just keep telling myself accidents happen.

PARTY CIRCUIT

I'd noticed that the classes were so small in the new school that all the kids get invited to the birthday parties. Today, it's official. Andrew is on the party circuit. At our last school, Andrew only got invited to one birthday party the entire time we were there. This year alone, we had already attended four parties, and we were only two months into the school year. After school today, Andrew came running to the car. While climbing in the car, he handed me a party invitation. "Look, Mom, I got invited to a birthday party for a kid in another class. Another class, Mom! He really wants to be my friend. He didn't have to invite me, I'm not even in his class." I wanted to cry. The good kind of cry. The happy cry. He really is doing it.

I knew that this was such a superficial measure of success, but I knew it meant he was fitting in. Andrew even understood that this meant he was fitting in, that kids like him. It may take him longer, but I just knew he was going to accomplish all that he set out to do. Changing schools was no easy task for him, but it was worth it. All the months of planning, strategizing, worrying, advice seeking, and pep-talking has paid off. I asked him if he wanted me to go to this party with him or just drop him off. "You know, Mom, I think I've got this one."

"You know what, Andrew, I think you do, too."

In all the nights that I laid awake worrying about him, I never could have imagined that he would want me to just drop him off. This was definitely a year of change. For the first time, I mean that in a good way.

NAMASTE

Andrew wanted to take karate lessons. I was shocked that he had any interest, for a kid that has such trouble balancing. I asked if he wanted to take karate because he thought he was going to be fighting like a ninja, to which he said no. He told me that he wanted to take karate to work on his balance and focus. What? How old is this kid? I found a karate studio that was close to home that offered a program I thought he could manage. They were only too happy to accommodate Andrew and his needs.

As always, Andrew loved to get a new uniform, and was wearing it in the car on the way home. He ran into the house and upstairs to practice with the video that they sent home with him. I was actually pleased to see him expand his areas of interest beyond baseball and Legos. This was quite an improvement, and it would keep him physically and mentally challenged. I only hoped that he liked it. I liked that while he was in a class with other kids, it was primarily a self-paced program. The kids didn't interact in a spontaneous way due to the structure of the classes. I peeked in to watch him practicing with the video. He stopped what he was doing and looked right at me (yes, eye contact) and said, "Mom, Namaste."

To which I responded, "Namaste, son."

I walked off very pleased that all on his own, he had found something that he was interested in doing, that would challenge him yet improve him physically and mentally. For years people had suggested karate to me, and I'm not even sure why I resisted. It's even better for Andrew that he came to the decision on his own. I thought he would take more pride in his successes if he could own the activity, not with something he had to do, something he wanted to do. Namaste.

NEUROSURGEON

It took us 18 months to get an appointment to consult the neurosurgeon. I was so hopeful that Andrew would be a candidate for surgery. I would love to see an end to the seizures for him. In order to get the appointment, we had to deliver all his records to her office for review, before she would even let us know if she would see him for a consult. The scheduler let me know that this consultation was in no way an indicator that Andrew would be taken on as a patient.

I had learned over the years that the harder it is to get an appointment, the more I trust what they had to say. Our appointment time was limited, as the doctor was scheduled for surgery that afternoon. I was sure that Andrew's anxiety over this appointment was directly correlated to mine. My stress level was palpable. The doctor had a difficult time engaging Andrew. Finally, she said to him, "Look Andrew, this is your brain, and your life. I need you to participate in this appointment. If you aren't interested, why should I be?" From that point on the two of them didn't even need me there.

After she conducted what appeared to be a physical exam, she told him that she wanted to ask him a few math questions. She said to him, "I see here that you are struggling with your math facts. I'd like to ask you a few questions. Would you like paper and a pencil?"

Andrew crossed his arms and slid back into his chair and replied coolly, "That won't be necessary." She asked him three difficult word problems that required him to complete complex math. At the conclusion she said to me that there is absolutely nothing wrong with his ability to use multiplication. He may not be able to regurgitate his multiplication tables on demand, but he has an advanced ability to use multiplication.

Then she turned to Andrew and said, "Andrew, you can let your teacher know that I'm one of the best at what I do in this country, and I can't do my multiplication tables. It's okay, that's what calculators are for." Andrew looked at me and smiled.

She let me know that she was willing to take Andrew on as a patient. He needed some further tests, but it looked like he was going to be a candidate for surgery. Relief washed over me. Short of growing out of the epilepsy, this surgery was his shot at an independent life. In the car on the way back home, I suggested to Andrew that he keep the surgeon's admission regarding multiplication tables to himself. "Your teacher may not appreciate what she had to say," I informed Andrew. Not to mention we had an entire school year left in her classroom.

Some things are better just kept to ourselves. Andrew told me at bedtime tonight that he was scared at the thought of having surgery. I told him we still had a lot of testing to do, and nothing had been decided yet. If we decided to have surgery, he would have a lot of time to get used to the idea. Then he asked the million-dollar question, "Mom, are you trying to fix me?"

I could barely croak out an answer. "Son, I love you just the way you are. I want you to have all the opportunities in life that you deserve. If there is a way to stop the seizures with surgery, then I want you to have surgery. I want only the best for you, the best life you can have. I just want to stop the seizures. I don't want to change you. I don't want to fix you. There is nothing to fix."

NEW SUIT

We had so many events that year that I told Andrew we had to go suit shopping. Lucky for me he likes to get dressed up. He was actually looking forward to getting a new suit. With any shopping trip I'd have to lay out the schedule of where we were going, and what we were doing. The girls were staying home with our nanny, Miss Hope, so I told him after we got the suit, I'd take him to Nordstrom for a tie and we'd have dinner there, just the two of us.

Immediately upon arrival at the suit store, Andrew let me know that he would really like two suits, one black and one gray. Yes, only my son would want not just one suit, but two. "Options, Mom," he informed me. He is definitely my son. As I was paying for the suits, the sales clerk began talking to Andrew about ties. She showed him all his options and he told her he didn't like any of them, which was fine with me because we already had a plan. Very loudly she informed me that there was a discount store nearby that sold children's ties. She actually wrote down directions to the store for me.

As soon as we walked out, I walked over to the garbage can and threw away the directions. Andrew started immediately with, "We're going to Nordstrom, right? You promised I could get my tie from Nordstrom. I don't want to go to that other store."

I calmly waited for him to quit talking. "Andrew, we're going to Nordstrom for your tie." The entire twenty-minute drive to Nordstrom, he was obsessed about getting the tie at Nordstrom. Was I sure I was driving the right way? Was Nordstrom going to be open by the time we got there? Could I drive faster? Was Nordstrom going to have any ties by the time we got there? The only question I had was, can I get a drink at Nordstrom? After twenty minutes of this mental gymnastics, I needed it.

Finally, I quit trying to reassure him. He had worked himself into this illogical circle of thoughts regarding the tie, and I knew it wouldn't matter what I said; we just had to get the tie. Just like the suits, we ended up with two ties. Options, you know. There were so few things that Andrew asked for in life, that when the opportunity presents itself I suppose I overdo it. Just like the Legos, we were now starting to acquire suits and ties. Deep in my heart, I knew it could be a lot worse. Not to mention, in some way, it made me feel better. I was overcompensating for all the things in his life that I couldn't make better or couldn't control. More Legos? Another suit? You bet, it's the least I can do.

NEW COACH

Today was the first day of practice for Andrew's new baseball season. There would be a new coach, new kids, new fields. It should be interesting to see how he adapts to all the changes. Today's practice was held at the batting cages, somewhere even I have never been before. I waited patiently to talk to Andrew's coach before I dropped him off for practice. I gave the coach the whole laundry list of concerns with Andrew. Remember, full disclosure is my new policy. The coach looked me right in the eye and said, "I have Parkinson's. I know what it's like to be different. I know what it's like to have limitations. Thank you for telling me, and trusting me with your son. He will be in good hands for the season." I felt good leaving Andrew there. Sometimes people are put in your life at the right time for all the right reasons. I know that Andrew is going to learn a lot this season, not just about the game of baseball. This is going to be a season where I'm not going to have to worry about how the other kids are treating Andrew. I know there is someone that gets him, that's looking out for him. A coach like this has the ability to teach Andrew beyond the fundamentals of baseball. He has the ability to teach my son about self-worth and self-preservation in the face of adversity, a lesson not lost on my son, who recognizes he is different. I will be forever grateful for this season and for such a truly great "coach."

CHECKING IN

Steve, Andrew and I were checking in when Andrew's dad arrived at the hospital. Andrew was checking in for a week-long stay for testing. His dad volunteered to stay the first two nights with Andrew, and I stayed the remainder of the week. The technician who was gluing the electrodes onto Andrews scalp was the same one that did it last time. He remembered Andrew. I spent the day getting Andrew comfortable and acclimated to the idea of being in the hospital for the week. It was hard for me to leave Andrew at the end of that first day. It just seemed so wrong to be going home without him. I didn't realize that he would be staying in the critical care unit. As prepared as I thought I was for this visit, it all became very serious to me.

By the end of the first day, the doctor let us know that Andrew would not be a candidate for surgery. His seizures came from more than one area of the brain. The concern was that the EEG was so abnormal, considering all the medication that he takes. The decision had been made to take him off his current meds and try something different. By the time it was my turn to stay with Andrew, I was looking forward to having him all to myself. I shared his bed with him and we watched movies non-stop, occasionally interrupted for Andrew to play some video games, which he now had the motor skills to enjoy, and to ride the stationary bike. I had the pleasure of being on duty the night that they wanted to run some tests while Andrew was in a sleep-deprived state. No one could possibly have been more sleep-deprived than me. I hadn't slept the entire week leading up to all this testing. Andrew really looked forward to the therapy dog visits each day. These dogs even have their own trading cards. One of the big dogs climbed up into bed with Andrew. He loved it. He actually enjoyed the therapy dogs more than when baseball players from the Los Angeles Angels of Anaheim came to visit him. Walking the hallways of the hospital made me thankful for the problems we have. We aren't fighting cancer, he hasn't lost a limb, he isn't in a coma, and he isn't fighting for his life. Sadly, I saw two families around me lose their children while we were there that week. I had the pleasure of leaving the hospital with the child I checked in with. Never in my life was I so thankful. On Sunday, I dropped the kids off at a party. Starting my car to drive home, my hands began to shake and I started to cry uncontrollably. I thought maybe I was experiencing symptoms of post-traumatic stress syndrome. That past week was the most stressful week of my life. I kept my game face on all week. As scared and sad as I was, no one would have known. It was so hard to watch all the testing that Andrew went through. If I could trade places with him, I would. While I was disappointed with the outcome of the hospital stay, Andrew had changed medications, and hopefully we would have more success on this one. Andrew amazed me all week. He didn't complain once. He never asked when he could go home. He only had one request all week; a meatball sub from Subway. Anything for my nice boy. Anything.

MISSION: BAR MITZVAH

This was our second trip to the East Coast, so I had bigger aspirations for this trip. Steve's nephew Joshua was having his bar mitzvah. I figured there would be plenty of boys at this function, and it was my goal to see if I could get Andrew to participate in all the activities. He wanted to go to the Friday night service, and I even heard him trying to chant Hebrew. I left early with the baby, and when Steve arrived back at the hotel with everyone, he said that Andrew had done a fantastic job.

I noticed that he was having a lot of problems controlling his tics, but he kept assuring me that he felt fine. The next morning during the service at the synagogue Andrew had a seizure, and just slid into a sleep recovery period. This is the time right after a seizure where the brain is recovering from the seizure itself. It typically can last for five minutes up to thirty minutes. I just sat with him and let his head rest on my shoulder. I was sure that everyone thought that Andrew was sleeping through the service.

I whispered to Steve that if he hadn't come around by the end of the service I needed to get Andrew to a doctor. He was so funny, he informed me that the synagogue had to be full of doctors, and that finding one when the service was over would be no problem. Andrew slowly but surely came to. I took him back to the hotel to lay down and sleep it off. I offered to stay behind with Andrew, but he really wanted to go to the party. Who could blame him? The party could be overwhelming for anyone, but I think he handled it nicely. He seemed to want to play the games but stayed away from the loud music. I kept a close eye on him all night. He was even reluctant to leave at the end of the party. As an objective observer, I thought Andrew stayed on the peripheral of all the activities. He didn't want to be right in the middle of anything. He just wanted to watch the action. He truly seemed to enjoy himself at a great event. I think that travel and the unknown is very difficult for Andrew. It may be difficult for a lot of people, actually. All in all, seizure aside, I have to say the trip was a success.

LOOKING FORWARD TO FOURTH

The bar was set extremely high for Andrew this year, and I am proud to say, he did it. He excelled academically, even in Andrew Standard Time. This year he showed tremendous progress in his pragmatic language skills. He was advanced in reading and math. He excelled in science and social studies; both subjects he loves. All three kids won the Nobel Prize this year in their respective science classes. I appreciated that Andrew was in an environment that fostered academic success and valued creative thinking.

The speech therapist at the school used Andrew as a leader in her cooking speech program. Little did she know that Andrew loves to cook and was perfect for the job. The Study Buddy program gave Andrew the extra attention that he needed for getting his schoolwork done. It was also an opportunity for Andrew to work on his social skills.

While I wouldn't say that he made a meaningful friendship this year, I think he was well liked. He certainly got invited to a lot of birthday parties. I chaperoned all of his field trips, and while he preferred to hang around with me, he seemed friendly and talkative with his peers. (I even managed to make a friend this year.) He tried new interests, while still holding onto some of the old ones.

He didn't have any problems on the playground, and I attributed that to the supervision and absolute clarity of the rules of the games. I think they call the program Peaceful Playgrounds. He certainly had more than his fair share of medical problems this year, but he took it all in stride. I noticed that he was trying to spend more time playing by himself at home, and I was giving him more space than I have in the past.

While Andrew still remained a bit of a management challenge, he was still the nicest boy ever. He would give his sisters or me his last cookie or the shirt off his back without blinking. Life remains full of challenges for Andrew, but he is looking forward to fourth grade with unwavering optimism.

FOURTH GRADE (AGE 9)
2012

BACK TO SCHOOL BBQ

As the kids climbed in the car at pick up, Andrew handed me a folded up piece of notebook paper. My first thought was, *Are you kidding me? Already a note from the teacher!!* Very calmly I asked, "What's this?"

"It's my new friend Gui's (his name is pronounced GEE) phone number." If I haven't mentioned it before, my kids go to the United Nations of elementary schools.

For summer vacation, Sophia had one classmate going to Switzerland (the mother informed me they alternate between Switzerland and Brazil each year), another going to Paris, two families going together to the Olympics in England, one to Hawaii for the summer and last, but not least, one to Egypt. In Isabella's class, four families were going on a two-week Italian holiday. These were just the plans I gathered through casual conversation. I digress—back to Andrew.

Andrew said Gui asked for his phone number but he didn't remember it. What? Seriously? He didn't remember my phone number?? At least every other day I ask him, "What's our phone number? What's our address?" I know that he doesn't know our address, but he at least knows the name of our neighborhood. But our phone number? I have a card in his backpack with all of this on it, in case he forgets and he didn't even remember that he had the information at his fingertips. Anyway, moving on...I said, "I'll call Gui's mom after you pick up your room."

Have I mentioned that Andrew is a hoarder? The entire ten-minute ride home he was obsessed. "When are you calling Gui's mom?"

"That all depends on how long it takes you to clean your room," I replied every time he asked me. Two hours later we left for the Back To School BBQ. I had not called Gui's mom, nor was the aforementioned bedroom picked up. Now he was obsessing the entire drive back to school about whether Gui would be at the BBQ.

Honestly, I was not looking forward to over managing four kids at basically a carnival on the blacktop. We parked, and I got everyone in sync with the plan. We got our food and headed to a picnic table. As I got everyone settled, I began to stuff my face with nachos, my guilty pleasure. I am not kidding when I tell you, cheese was everywhere, including under my perfectly manicured fingernails. I am in foodie heaven when, guess who walks up? Yep, Gui and his parents. I can't even shake their hands due to my cheese indulgence, and not a napkin within a one-mile radius. I mean, who planned this thing? Food trucks, kids, snow cones, cake and no napkins? I had to assume the planner was one of the many moms with a full-time staff and the napkin thing, well just a detail…anyway, as embarrassed as I was, Gui's parents did all the talking. They were new to the area :) Live in our neighborhood :) And the best part, would LOVE to have Andrew over. Best Day Ever. This couldn't have gone any better.

We exchanged phone numbers and as they walked away, the uneasiness descended. Do I tell them? How can I not? Will they still want to have Andrew over? Maybe not? Will they be able to tell? Could he do it just this once? I didn't know. My conscience told me, remember the last time you did this without telling the parents. Story involved a broken tooth, and not Andrew's. UGGGGHHHH. Anyway, I'd have plenty of time to worry about that, since I was sure it would take a few days for them to call me.

BLOOD WORK

The new medication required frequent blood tests, which I hate. Certainly better than the old days, when I would have to hold him down. He now has a fascination with how all the tests work. He liked to ask a lot of questions, and he liked to watch. Steve took all the girls to school for me today so I could get Andrew over to the lab for his blood work. If he behaves appropriately, he knows he gets to get a Lego set of some kind. I was pushing the architectural buildings. He's already earned the Space Needle.

We arrived at the lab when it opened at 7:30 a.m. and were fifth in line. As usual, Andrew was a trooper. As we were leaving the lab and before we got to the waiting area, I heard him say softly, "Mom, I think I'm in trouble." He looked as if he was going to pass out. I set him in a chair and got him a glass of water. The woman who worked at the lab came out to make sure he was okay. She suggested going next door and getting him something to drink and eat. I carried him next door and grabbed a chocolate milk for him to get started on while I ordered him a bagel. By the time he finished eating, he was already looking better.

The entire drive back to school, he wanted to talk about how he almost fainted. In all his years of having blood taken, we had never had an experience like this. I told him maybe he shouldn't watch. He thinks it happened because they took too much blood. He informed me that they usually don't take that many vials. Isn't it funny? I didn't even know what they take. I was just hoping to get it over with without incident.

As I signed him in at school, he informed me that maybe this time he should get two Lego sets, since he "almost passed out, you know." Yes, Andrew, you can have two Lego sets. I would give anything if I didn't have to take him for blood work in the first place. The least I can do is offer up two Lego sets. I just chalk it up to the cost of doing business.

WHERE AM I?

I loved Andrew's fourth-grade teacher. She was a former kindergarten teacher who, before becoming a teacher, was an Emergency Medical Technician. Kind and capable: a dangerous combination. Not to mention beautiful. Andrew really responded well to the pretty ladies.

I received a phone call from her today that she was concerned with Andrew's lethargy in the afternoons. He had started laying down on his desk. Andrew is a lot of things, but he has never been so tired that he lays on his desk. He has always followed the rules of the classroom. He always knows what is expected of him. After we talked strategy, she lobbed a grenade. Yesterday, while he was being observed, Andrew returned from the restroom and didn't know where he was. He muttered, "Where am I?" I let her know that is symptomatic of his seizures, and that I would call his doctor immediately. I asked her to please call me if it happened in the future and I would come down and pick him up. That's exactly why he was laying down on his desk. I immediately called Dr. Donnelly's office and left a voicemail. I couldn't even leave a message without crying. My poor boy. The new medication wasn't working either. How could I expect him to learn anything when he was having seizures throughout his school day?

I felt so helpless, so frustrated. Dr. Donnelly called me right back. We were adding to Andrew's medication, and he was going to schedule an EEG and an MRI. We were starting the cycle of worry all over again. All I hoped was that we could get it scheduled this calendar year, since I'd already met my insurance deductible. That was the only bright side to it all.

NOTE TO SELF

Note to self: I am doing what I am supposed to be doing, and sometimes that is more important than what I want to be doing.

I WOULDN'T HAVE IT ANY OTHER WAY

I used to worry obsessively about, "What will become of Andrew if something happens to me?" The truth was: I don't know what would have become of me without Andrew. I have learned more and will continue to learn more from Andrew than he will ever learn from me. I see the world so differently through his eyes. Andrew has taught me the true meaning of unconditional love. He loves me just the way I am. He sees the best in humanity, yet uses discernment when necessary.

My son is the first one to share whatever he has, and the last one to ask for anything. He is the bravest person I know. His spirit is undefeatable. He never lets anything get him down, and never complains.

Life is not easy for Andrew, and he faces many challenges. But to him, it's just the way life is. He is truly the peacemaker at home. Andrew will try anything to keep the peace, from giving up his treat, to allowing the TV channel to be changed, trying a joke, or just giving someone words of encouragement. It's Andrew who has created the optimist in me. He inspires me to look for the best in every situation, seeing every challenge as an opportunity for growth.

Every day I do my best to be the person he can count on to help him achieve his every dream. While my hopes and dreams for Andrew are always changing and ever-evolving, one thing I hold close to my heart is the knowledge that he is destined for great things. In my darkest hour I never lost hope. I know that we face many challenges and opportunities for growth ahead of us, but if Andrew can do it with a positive attitude, I have no excuse. If I had known all that I know now about what life would be like raising a child like Andrew, I still wouldn't have had it any other way.

I HAVE A DREAM

I have a dream for you, Andrew.

I want you to be all that you can be. I have high expectations for you because I believe you can achieve anything your mind dreams.

You have a brilliant mind and I want you to use it to achieve great things. You see the world in a way that no one else does.

My dream is for you to become an amazing scientist or doctor and use your fantastic mind to heal people.

You are the nicest boy I know. You have a gentle spirit about you. You are kind and loving. The way you treat your friends, family, and even strangers makes me proud.

My dream is for you to continue to treat everyone you meet with the respect and dignity that they deserve. To have an open heart and a forgiving spirit. You have the amazing gift of discernment. Don't ever lose this. It will help you to know good people from bad. Use this special gift to protect yourself.

Use all of your special gifts to make this world a better place. You are an unbelievable young man. You have touched the lives of many people in a profound way. Make them all proud that they know you, Andrew. You have changed my life. I have learned more from you, son, than you will ever learn from me.

It is my job to help you achieve your dreams, Andrew and I want you to know, I believe in YOU!

I love you, son,
XO

Mom